PROFESSIONAL

EVENT

PLANNING

A Complete Skill-Building Guide

Mandy Adebayo, PhD

First edition, © 2012.

A paperback edition of this book was originally published in 2012 by M.O. Press, Kaduna. Orders for the copy can be addressed to Movina Managers Limited. It is distributed with the title: The Professional Event Planner: Develop Your Event Management Skills, be the Event Planner

info@movinamanager.org

+2348033112590 | +2348099587425

© 2024 by Mandy Adebayo, PhD.

ISBN:

Print: 979-8-3305-0148-9

E-book: 979-8-3305-0149-6

The second edition is published under title: Professional Event Planning: A Complete Skill-Building Guide. The first edition was revised and updated.

Front Page Graphic credits; Freepik.com.

Author

Mandy Adebayo, PhD.

mandyadebayo68@gmail.com

+2348033112590 | +2348099587425

Dedication

For my beloved husband, who has been my constant source of strength and inspiration. Your love makes everything possible.

Acknowledgment

A special thank you to my family, for the countless hours of support and encouragement. You have been my rock through it all. I want to also say thank you to my readers—you are the reason this book exists, and I am eternally grateful for your support.

Table of contents

Preface

As I sat down to update the first edition of this book, "The
Professional Event Planner," I couldn't help but reflect on the
countless moments of joy, connection, and inspiration that events have
brought into my life. All events are precious to us and are filled with
memories, whether they are personal get-togethers with loved ones or
grand celebrations that bring communities together.

Having worked in the thrilling field of event planning for over 20
years, I have had the honour of personally experiencing the
transformational effect of a well-executed event. I've also gone
through the difficulties, disappointments, and uncertain times that
come with the job.

It's from this place of experience, passion, and dedication that I offer
this book as a guide and companion to fellow event planners, both
seasoned professionals and aspiring newcomers alike. Within these
pages, you will find a wealth of knowledge, insights, and practical
advice gleaned from years of planning events of all sizes and colours.

But more than just a manual of techniques and strategies, this book is
a testament to the artistry, creativity, and resilience that define the
world of event planning. It is a celebration of the countless
individuals who work tirelessly behind the scenes to bring events to life
and create unforgettable experience for clients and guests.

You embark on your journey through the pages of this second edition
now "Professional Event Planning: A Complete Skill Building Guide,"
I encourage you to approach each chapter with an open mind and a
spirit of curiosity. Embrace the challenges, seize the opportunities, and
allow yourself to be inspired by the endless possibilities that await you
in the world of event planning.

Whether you're planning your first event or looking to take your skills
to the next level, remember that you are not alone. We are part of a

vibrant community of event planners, each with our own unique perspectives, talents, and stories to share,

So, with excitement and anticipation, I invite you to join me on this journey of exploration, discovery, and growth. Together, let us unlock the secrets of professional event planning and create experiences that will leave a lasting impact on the world around us.

Mandy Adebayo (PhD)

Introduction

Every event planner organizes events meaning they have to reliably meet the responsibility of their assignment. It is not possible to become an event planner overnight. People who want to become architects realize that they have about six or more years of schooling ahead of them, before they can be one. People who want to become president of companies know that they need to work for many years within that company or within that industry, and learn it from the ground up. In event planning this attitude is imperative. You cannot as a planner, work out the timing of a major event, unless you have worked several events and have seen what works, and what doesn't.

Every business satisfies a set of people within the business community and event planning is not left out. Planners work long and non-traditional hours to plan and execute all details related to a variety of meeting formats including seminars, conferences, incentive, golf events and other programmes. The bottom line is you have to learn the ropes and put in your time in order to succeed in the future.

There is no single business that can thrive beyond its ability to meet needs; keeping abreast of this fact is very important to event planners.

Event planning is more than just catering for an event or decorating the event space. It is a multifarious business built on trust and reliability and requires fresh creative concepts. Successful planning ensures that an organization/event remains competitive.

In contemporary times guests expect their events to be more exciting and scintillating; they cannot get that easily without the planner been trendy. This book in your hand is a work tool for everyone in event business who wants to increase knowledge including entrants. What you know gives confidence and makes it possible for you to respond to assigned tasks. Positioning at the market place determines how much you make in this business industry; this is why "constant change" is inevitable for event planners. The only one who can effect a desired change is you and change comes only by what we know to do and do correctly. How much you are willing to know depends on you. That you have been planning events for long does not exempt you from acquiring new ideas that can lead to greatness. No matter how much we know in any area there are always new things to learn and things we have previously learned that we need to be refreshed in.

Whether you're a seasoned professional or embarking on a new career path, this book is your roadmap to success in the dynamic and exhilarating world of event management.

Events hold a unique power to inspire, connect and leave a lasting impact on those who attend. From weddings and corporate gatherings to concerts and conferences, each event presents an opportunity to create unforgettable experiences that bring people together and celebrate life's special moments.

As an event planner, you are not simply a coordinator of logistics; you are a creator of memories, a visionary, and a master of transformation. With meticulous attention to detail and boundless creativity, you have the power to turn dreams into reality and exceed the expectations of your clients and guests.

In the pages that follow, you will embark on a journey through the fundamental principles, best practices, and innovative strategies that define professional event planning. From understanding your client's vision to navigating logistics, designing experiences, managing risk, and leveraging technology, each chapter is designed to equip you with the knowledge and skills needed to thrive in this exciting industry.

It is important we know how to enhance productivity level in this industry. This is a fast track to everyone who diligently wants proficiency and excellence in event planning business, don't be a mediocre for another second. When you read it cover to cover and apply what you have read, your professional skills necessary to reliably meet the responsibility of your assignment will get strengthened by the day.

It is time to throw your event planning into the right ring. Remember, event planners are being called upon to develop and stage literally millions of events each year; you could just be one of them.

When I started off two decades plus ago, I had so many questions to answer when I have opportunity to introduce myself as an event planner. The situation got so daunting when l couldn't find on any book shelf any single material on this field authored by a Nigerian for the Nigerian teeming event planning industry.

I often hear people say "who is an event planner and what does an event planner do?" This and other questions necessitated my writing this book and have been invaluable to readers.

Whether you are called to plan a gala dinner, exhibitions, benefit concerts, fundraising events, festivals, conferences and workshops to name just a few, it seems rather difficult at times due to their complexities and importance. The need to have the basics cannot be overemphasized. This is why this book is timely and relevant at a time like this when knowledge has become so important in modern technological business environment.

The information herein is great ideas and useful insights that will culminate in your success as a professional event planner. Knowing what to do is a step to success but no matter how much you know in any area there are always new things to learn and things we have previously learned that needs to unlearned.

Chapter One

Event at a glance

Event is a planned short – term activity undertaken in a building or series of buildings or structure or series of structures covering an area of defined open land where a group of persons come together for a specific purpose at whatever time. In this context "event" is a planned social occasion, it is simply process of researching, planning and ensuring the smooth organization or flow of event.

Event planning is a multi-billion Naira industry with distinct and organized program. It is any function with more than five people gathering for the purpose of celebration, education and marketing.

The type of position an event planner looks for determines the specific event the planner works at. This may include exhibitions, festivals, tradeshows, conferences, award events, holiday events, concerts, and workshops to mention a few.

Goldblatt, 2005 defined event as "a unique moment in the celebrated with ceremony and ritual to satisfy specific needs."

In essence, every individual or corporate organization organizes events at one time or the other and it can be scheduled to happen anywhere, any day and anytime. Events are borne under varied circumstances. An event can be centred on a special occasion such as birthday, anniversary or wedding celebration. A fashion show, benefit concert or art show can become an event. In the business world, entertaining clients, recruiting new employees and holiday celebration can all constitute events. But all events are not created equal. Each event differs in time commitment to plan and execution. But whatever the motive for the event, care needs to be taken in the planning stages. To effectively plan and execute, event can be classified into different groups namely - educational and informative these include workshops and meetings. Some events are geared towards raising funds, such as festivals, concert, holding a raffle or an auction, while others are people focused event such as preliminary events, weddings and the like. Events can either be big or small; it can be cantered on business, marketing or leisure.

Different organizations stage events for a variety of reasons:

- Promoters stage events such as jazz, festivals, and concerts to make a profit
- Businesses stage events like retreats, product launches and tradeshows to increase sales and promote products
- Tourism organizations stage events to attract visitors, extend their length of stay and generate return visitors
- Governments stage events such as democracy day to promote special occasions
- Charities stage events to raise funds and profile.
- It is necessary to ascertain the cause of the event in the planning stages.

The difficult task is to select the activity that best serves the objectives and to produce the event with zeal and skill so that it can contribute to the building of the community.

Events start slowly at preparation and as the event date nears, the workload builds up until the day when planners are busy running about to make sure everything goes well. If this is not properly managed, then you burn out and if you fail to manage the pressure appropriately you make bad decisions.

Importance of events

- Events can provide the means for a flow of money and recognition into a community that would not have otherwise occurred.
- Events provide opportunity for new experiences, learning and enjoyment
- Events may have an indirect impact as direct spending leads to further rounds of spending, income generation and employment

- A direct impact on local economy through direct spending by visitors may be another importance
- In addition to economic impact, events can have a positive impact socially and culturally. Events provide opportunity for people to interact one with another, helping to create a sense of belonging and social cohesion.

Getting an event off the ground and completing it successfully is a feather in your cap, gets you repeat clients and ensures good business.

Understanding the professional event planner

Event planning is an authentic knowledge – based service that cannot be replaced by modern contraptions and planners require professionalism to efficiently plan and manage event projects. Who then is a professional? A professional is someone who claims to possess knowledge of something and has a commitment to a particular code or set of values, both of which are fairly well accepted characteristics of the profession. Being a professional means being an expert. It means being competent and skilful, it also means behaving in an ethical manner. It means putting your clients first and acting in the best interest of the public or society. It is about being reliable, trustworthy and committed. Do you know in some major hotel chains the upper management all have to first work for a week in every department of the hotel? Event planners are masterminds behind the large and small details of social and corporate event. It means "the Planner" is an expert who has to first acquire all the nitty-gritty of event planning in other to get an in-depth knowledge of the industry at large. This is the only way that person can truly understand how Event planning works, from the inside out. If you take that attitude toward your Event planning career, one can only step back and watch you succeed. In Event planning this attitude is imperative. You cannot as an Event planner, work out the timing of a major event, unless you've worked several events and have seen what works and what doesn't.

Professionalism encompasses a number of attributes and together those attributes identify and define a professional.

What are these attributes?

- Specialized knowledge
- Competency
- Honesty and Integrity

They never compromise their values. If a project falls outside their scope of expertise, they're not afraid to admit this. They ask for help from others when they need it and they're willing to learn from others.

- Accountability
- Self-regulation: Genuine professional shows respect for the people around them. They don't let a bad day impact how they interact with clients.
- Image: They look the part. They are polished and dress appropriately for the situation. They exude an air of confidence and they gain respect for this.

Having known who a professional is, the professional Event planner is thus a man or woman who organizes, sets up and manages various corporate, public and private events and meetings ethically. Event planners get things done through other people. Hence using an Event planner has a particular advantage in finding choice details of an event because they usually have established working relationships with exceptional vendors. As an Event planner, you'll have a large responsibility in planning the perfect event for your clients. They can often work out deals that aren't available to others. She does not only find appropriate vendors, but negotiates dates, time and rates. They also develop budget and determine the need for food, drinks and equipment. They make decisions, allocate the client's resources and direct the activities of service providers and suppliers to attain goals. They ensure that caterers can plan and accommodate special meals and diets for all classes of people and their needs. An Event planner has the capacity to coordinate every aspect of the event including the caterer. They can evaluate meal choices, prepare for special diets and coordinate all little details so that every element of the event is congruent with each other.

Many professional planners actually attend the conventions, meetings or concerts they organize in order to ensure that all of the attendees' needs are met. A professional Event planner is responsible for planning and coordinating a variety of events for corporations, nonprofit organizations and individuals. In other words, the planner can take the stress off clients by assuming all of the duties involved with planning and executing an event.

The professional Event planner is a highly specialized person who handles every detail of an event. She is usually called upon to develop and stage literally thousands of events everywhere and every-time.

For easy understanding, she is the builder, painter and gluer that take all the pressure off clients by multitasking on several things at one time, face numerous deadlines and orchestrate the activities of many diverse groups of people so clients can do what they are supposed to be doing like dinning, hosting, greeting, mingling and having a great time.

She is the point person or principal source of information that moves the event activities and at the same time makes sure that all the little details of the events such as initial planning, preparing a budget, deciding a theme for themed events, site selection, entertainment, reviewing proposals, negotiating discounts, planning menu, coordinating publicity, obtaining volunteers, choosing speakers and arranging the programme down to presenting the organization's information in the most effective way. She does not just plan events but also manages and execute the event thereby taking responsibility for the creative, technical and logistical elements.

Some services offered by event management companies are given below:

1. A perfect atmosphere
2. Promotional activities
3. Providing other amenities
4. Service package
5. Public impact

Event planners are in charge of all details that go into planning and execution of the entire event from the moment the idea for an event is conceived, right down to clean – up when the last attendee has left the event.

They may be involved in the following:

- development of a planning schedule
- budget development and management
- theme creation and development
- vendor selection and liaising
- menu selection
- contract negotiation
- Selecting and arranging gifts
- Prizes and premiums
- Guest list management
- Arranging travel and lodging

The more you practice the tenets of this business the more proficient you become in the field. The bottom line is the benefit the planner derives is proportional to the activities she carries out. Major responsibilities therefore include active participation, interaction, critical evaluation and effective communication.

People have been providing event planning services since the beginning of modern man and may be even before then. There is the Biblical project on creation in the first book of the Holy Bible, how that God in six days created the world out of a negative situation. There were specific projects for each day and the time frame for this gigantic project was six days of working and evaluation. Then a day was set aside for rest after schedules have been executed.

Another project in the Holy Bible that can be seen as a major event is the removal of the ark from the house of Obededom to the house of King David and the feeding of the entire populace with bread, cake, a good piece of flesh and flagon of wine by the king. These were milestone events, well planned and well organized.

However, anyone who has to put up such a gathering knows it is anything but easy and effortless. Not even the smallest detail is left to chance.

As a teenager growing up in one of the States in Nigeria, I remembered the passing of a king. In the period between the death of the old king and the coronation of the new king different activities took place that included dance troupes and masquerades coming to the palace from within and outside the town and this went on for days with great pageantry. I believe someone was responsible for heading the committee that was involved in arranging such a unique event and managing the crowd. I will never be able to say if the organizers got rewarded then for their services or not. But the proficiency to organize such events that look effortless, with precision and without strain depicts the job of an event planner. It is probably safe to assume that the basic organizational aspects of coordinating such great projects are still the same today. It is appropriate to find out what sort of people and organization require events and how best to satisfy them. This is because every successful event business takes people into cognizance. And every such event must have the following:

- Well defined vision
- Preliminary planning time
- Feasibility study
- Execution period
- Evaluation period

Planning time is actually thinking time and time should be scheduled for thinking on the project.

The professional planner has challenges to enjoy because it is a time consuming and stressful business. She loves to see the outstanding factor which is the big picture and want others to see it also. She is endowed with planning with precision and implementing the plans. In a nut shell, she simply organizes events by planning and executing and coordinating accordingly.

The planner is a key player in this rewarding industry. Specific event may require one event planner or more depending on the size and scope of the event. The scope of an event defines what the event is supposed to accomplish and the budget that has been created to achieve the set objectives. Any change to the scope of the project like increase in number of persons attending the event must be accompanied by approval for a change in budget and schedule. The scope must be clearly identified and associated to the time-line and budget.

Today, Event planners play a major role in every aspect of life. The reason been that the pressure of work on people have increased drastically and they are also incapable of organizing their events professionally. To meet up with the demands of work and society, the responsibility of articulating the activities of events and executing the events has to be given out to those who have experience. With people getting busier by the day, most of them are just too happy to shift the burden on someone else shoulders, even if they have to pay for it.

The Event planner is hired to advise, make decisions, allocate the clients resources; direct the activities of service providers and suppliers to attain desired goals. Anytime people gather together for a purpose, someone is needed to oversee all details to ensure the event happens and that it is a success.

To be more explicit Event planners and their team are often behind the scenes running every great event, analysing the event and managing it. These include overall design, audiovisual production, logistics, budgeting, negotiation and client service. They may be involved in the following:

1. Brand building
2. Event marketing
3. Event project management
4. Communication strategy
5. Establishing budget and monitoring
6. Branding
7. Providing constant progress update to clients

8.   On-site production from having the right idea to the
     completion of the event and the final tidying up the venue.

Chapter Two

Habits of successful event planners

These essentials are intertwined with everything an event planner does. Having these traits will enhance the performances of great event planners. We should cherish the advantages we therefore stand to derive.

a.   Staying organized with attention to detail

The success achieved for any event is in the details and research. To be a fine event planner, one must always be in good in planning and organizing events. Being organized is the buzz word that makes the event move smoothly. This is the reason event planners get themselves rolling. Organized event planners are able to think quickly and intelligently. Your planning and organizing skills will come in handy when dealing with a large number of people. If you are sure, you can handle all pressure and still able to plan and organize an event, then you are just right for the job.

Customers and companies are always looking for someone with good planning and organizing skills and whom they can rely on.

- They make and keep lists of all that the event entails from logistics planning to budget creation, concept design to contract negotiations and production.
- They are experts in filling receipts and balancing account books.
- They create a structured workplace.
- They manage their time better

Your organizational capabilities which are the main reason you are being hired will be tested from time to time. This means taking total control of all your event planning projects.

Organization

Success for any event is in the details. Although it takes plenty of creativity to design an event that is memorable and meaningful, it also takes careful attention to details, adaptability, effective delegating and lots of work. Event organization is key to achieving success. From logistics planning to entertainment, concept design to contract negotiations, every detail is organized to compliment your goals. Once you have decided what, where and when, it's time to work on details of an event. Coordinating event details is a time-consuming job that involves multitasking, particularly if you must organize several events simultaneously. The fundamental issue for organization as a basic managerial function is therefore, how to achieve a good co-ordination and cooperation among activities, functions, personnel so that the logistic objectives can be implemented effectively. You should be able to follow through activities to ensure they are being accomplished as planned and effecting corrections in any significant deviations. Using an event planner allows clients to concentrate and enjoy the actual event stress free.

The uniqueness of it all is that the event planner participates directly in the activities that produce the end result, and as well strives to maintain the progress and productive mutual interaction of various parties in such a way that overall risk of failure is reduced. They are at the foreground of event activities. Good organization is essential if you are to effectively handle event tasks simultaneously. As a successful event planner, you must establish structure and stability for each project. This is achieved by how much of the event has been researched, ability to identify the target audience, devising the event concept, planning the logistics and coordinating the technical aspects. All of these precede getting down to actually executing the modalities of the proposed event and above all taking all the worries away from people who use their services. In other words, good organizational skills enable you to complete all your assigned tasks and keep track of project deadlines. They also prevent unnecessary mistakes from occurring. This means control of all your event projects. An event planning notebook or binder will keep you organized. Regardless of your level of experience, you will create amazing business events if you stay organized along the way. Creating an event binder is probably the most efficient way to stay organized for planning seminars, conferences, internal trainings, executive meetings or other business events. The business generates a lot of paper work, many conversations and endless details.

Each project should have its own binder depending on the complexity of the event, it should include several sections:

- Itinerary/agenda
- Key contact
- Attendees
- Budget
- Communications
- Contracts
- Activities
- Banquet Event Orders
- Entertainment
- Miscellaneous
- Lodging/Rooming list
- Arrivals/Departures
- Gifts

The importance of being organized

- Greater ability to cope in a busy environment
- Being able to create order in life and work
- Ability to successfully handle several assignments at once
- Proper time management
- Being able to create a well- structured workplace.

b. Interpersonal relations

The Event planners genuinely like working with people which is a vital aspect of people's skills. This implies they have the ability to be friendly. At its core, event planning is about relationships, relationship with clients, relationship with suppliers and relationship with staff members. Your desire and ability to establish and maintain those relationships are vital to your success.

- The event planner love meeting, reading and working with people
- She initiates conversation and listen to what is being said calmly
- She can get others to efficiently work together with a common goal
- She is an expert in relationship building.

c.   Creativity

Being creative is the ability to see more than one side of an issue. This is critical to being able to describe, persuade, explain and convince others of your opinion. Those with this skill:

- Can paint a picture in someone's mind
- They can find unique ideas in unlikely place
- They can put things together that normally are not associated and get a pleasant effect.
- They are inquisitive to learn new things

This will be further elaborated on in subsequent chapter.

d.   Resourcefulness

This is a must have trait for planners. A resourceful event planner will have more than one solution to any given problem. If plan A does not work, they are ready with alternate plan B and C. Resourcefulness requires a "can do" attitude and a creative mind. The more you research on your available resources, the simpler it is to overcome any loopholes in objectives and pull together the perfect occasion.

Those with this trait:

- Seem to have boundless energy and enthusiasm to turn business ideas into reality

- They can do it themselves because they are the best choice
- They can make new things out of existing practice
- They can think outside the box and be professional working with great enthusiasm
- They are logical and innovative
- They give quality service to make a difference on client satisfaction.

e. Ability to take risk

- They are not afraid of considering the worst-case scenario when giving solutions to issues
- They are ready and able to take quick action to reduce loss
- They are able to discern between alternatives.
- They are calm, humorous and are able to comport themselves.

f. Enterprising

This is the process of identifying, developing and bringing a vision to life. Event planners can translate client's vision into reality. They have the courage to risk time, effort and money to achieve desired objective.

- They never exercise poor judgment
- They have integrity
- They are responsible
- They know no matter how tough it is running this business; they are sure of success.

g. They are good negotiators

Negotiating comes into at every stage of the Event planning process. Whether you're negotiating your fee with your clients or you're negotiating contracts with your suppliers, event planners should master the art of persuasion. Their goal is to have everyone included feel as though they have received a fair deal – a critical component to building lasting business relationship.

Chapter Three

Basic tools for success

Great event planners are addicted to studying to know more. A great passion for knowledge is never too much. What then do you require for an uncompromising success?

Knowledge of the industry

The greatest misunderstanding of man is to believe he understands everything. Knowledge is known as the information or awareness derived through experience or education. It is the sum of what you know about this business. The intensity of your knowledge depends on the intensity of your desire. This is a generation of information and knowledge is the currency of the world. Knowledge is the mastery of facts that gives strength to the one who acquires it; hence knowledge is the pacesetter for every business progress. Having this in mind, it therefore means you can't do without having an overview of this field you want to venture into or already into. For your business to stand the test of time and for you to become a successful entrepreneur in event planning you need sound and detailed knowledge of the industry.

A full knowledge of this business will spread fast the message of your uniqueness; it will benefit your business and validate evidence. These three constitute your unique selling proposition. The bottom line is, you should learn the ropes and put in your time now, in order to succeed in the future. Treat your "learning curve" as a fun internship, during which you still get to work great events. Learning something new every day in this career gives you an edge over your competitors. If you must see progress, then devote yourself to learning.

From a biblical point of view, Moses needed to be trained forty years for his assignment and for this he had a rod which can be likened to having the right tools that made him stand out and become extraordinary. The rod is creative and this is a pre-requisite to effectiveness and productivity. It goes beyond the normal class room degrees from colleges and tertiary institutions.

How much understanding has been acquired of the business and what effort are you making towards knowing better and acquiring new skills? It is not possible to get outstanding business results when operating the status quo that means doing business the same way over a period of time, without making necessary effort towards positive change. The quest for knowledge should not be passive and more so there are trends and fads to trade regularly. Change is impossible when you lack adequate prerequisite information. You must know what the business requires and ensure you are doing it appropriately.

When I started forth in 2003, the clientele was low since people needed to know my capabilities and build trust in me to handle such robust service, what I did was to get trained in an aspect of event planning that was more recognized way back then and kick started from there.

The whole truth is that knowledge should be treasured, only then can people crave for it. We all know that applied knowledge is power. Never let grass grow under your feet. When you stop growing in knowledge you start dying intellectually, spiritually, emotionally and professionally. With this end in view, to be tutored in necessary areas to achieve your goals cannot be overemphasized. Knowledge opens the door to life. Every door has a key and until the right key is located for the right door, shame is inevitable. Your business will have patronage when you start maybe by virtue of your influence in the society but what keeps it running over time is the knowledge you have attained. It is far too much a risk to the event project manager to have staff without the pre-requisite knowledge to handle event tasks.

In other words, one of the ways to acquire that productive power that can eliminate struggle is knowledge. You can also attain your great height through continuing education programs and seminars. To become eminent, you cannot rule out quality access to business information.

In essence, only adequate knowledge about this field can brighten the future of your colourful business. Sometimes we also need to be stirred up in things we already know. You can never know it all; this is actually the bane of most entrepreneurs. Have it in mind that the more you study the more credible you become.

Passion

Passion is the drive towards personal success. It fuels motivation.

Starting a business and running it successfully is the greatest desire of every Eventpreneur. Passion is not an obligation neither is it someone else's vision. It is something that flows from your inside. It is what you have a strong feeling for and love doing without been coaxed; it is what interest you and gives you a sense of fulfilment. Passion is not a privilege of the fortunate few. It is a competitive advantage that all in business can leverage. Having passion is not following the crowd but following your heart. There is nothing as great as earning a living doing what you love. Passion helps to turn good organization into great ones, it gives you fulfilment doing what you love every day of your life without grumbling. Passion should be a great ingredient in your business strategies. What does your organization have that makes it better than the competition? How does it distinguish itself in an increasingly complex and competitive economy? Does it exude enthusiasm to clients? Does it attract and retain high – performing staff and strategic partners? If not, then it may be missing out on the greatest competitive advantage an organization can claim. Passion is the competitive advantage that organizations can't buy. It can turn your small business into great one.

Having passion is not enough; pursuing it is what makes the difference. It is actually all about loving what you do. There is a direct correlation between passion and our potentials.

When you love your work, you become outstanding because the zeal to work whether convenient or not becomes a reality. Having passion means understanding value and creating culture. Having a viable culture that reflects your creed is very relevant to passionate

Eventpreneurs. With passion, patience, and experience comes great patronage, increased pay and respect. It fuels our strongest emotions.

Being a passionate event planning motivates, empowers, energizes and makes your footing firm. It invariably puts you ahead of others.

For entrants, I will advise you never go into Event planning because someone else is doing it, only love for Event planning can invigorate the creative and productive mind. For instance, we have many today, who are so called Event planners that have never been tutored and have no passion for the job. All they do is they have the contacts and then sub contract to people who can do the job for them without any single concept incorporated into the event by themselves. Some others are very good at reproducing what they see at any function. Commit yourself to it if is your passion and it will transcend conventional business practices. Passion will ensure that customers' expectations are not only met but exceeded.

There is fulfilment when an event planner is able to take her passion and build on it by continuing to learn, develop and improve on acquired skills. It is always good we balance it up because passion as important as it seem may not always create a successful event planning business. Commitment to continuous skill improvement and experience cannot be over-emphasized; these together can truly become unstoppable force in this business. Keep your passion a passion and not a burden. It means delegate tasks and assign responsibilities that don't "call to you" to other people.

Professional development and training

Professional development is investing one's energy and resources towards acquisition of relevant skills and competencies that will enable him/her achieve their personal career goals. It is concerned with the acquisition of new skills, knowledge and attitude that will prepare individuals for future job responsibilities.

Your number one asset in business is you the business owner. This is where having a mentor is major key, to give you the support to command the level that you are worth.

At least three basic components or core values serve as a conceptual basis and practical guideline for understanding the inner meaning of development. These core values are sustenance, self – esteem, and freedom, they represent common goals sought by all individuals and societies. Development is legitimized as a goal because it is an important, perhaps even an indispensable, way of gaining esteem, freedom and sustenance. Professional development is significant in driving the success of an event, acting to corroborate its effective delivery.

In the poorest village of Nigeria or even the wealthiest cities of the world, every human heart cries and yearns for the same thing: a chance to fulfil his or her dreams and desires. Even the poorest man has a dream. True freedom demands great responsibility, accountability, a spirit of stewardship, maturity, wisdom and character and all these are relevant in any business. This is the reason I separated professional development from business knowledge because in my few years in this field I've seen quite a knowledgeable group of persons who are not self -developed in the actual sense of it. When we are able to connect knowledge of the business with self - development we have a solid, stronger and unshakable business foundation that moves us higher. This to me is self - development in actuality. Irresponsibility is freedom deadliest enemy. Many in business fall prey to it. Having then decided that you have what it takes to be an Event planner, you really need to look at your educational background. Further education is an asset to give you more knowledge and credibility. Having a degree can give you an added advantage over others in this industry.

Qualification and vastness in all of the following fields could be advantageous if you consider efficiency and soundness:

    a.   Excellent Public Relations skills
    b.   Marketing skills
    c.   Degree in Business Administration
    d.   Strong Networking
    e.   Certificate / Diploma in Event Planning
    f.   Practical Life Experience

Beyond a quest for a degree program, continuing education courses
for professionals that can give Event planners the credentials they need
to fulfil their dream must be identified. Participation through at-home
learning, seminars and workshops cannot be overemphasized.
Seminars are worthless if you put another notebook on your shelf.
This is one major way to boost your curriculum vitae and convince
your clients easily and rapidly without many hassles. Have faith in
yourself and let it take you to the next level.

Though many independents don't have a formal education in our
society it doesn't rule out its importance, rather it is a prerequisite for
progress. Your educational prowess, practical experience and
knowledge can be your real asset. We all have natural unique ideas that
need to be re- enforced and worked out through the instrumentality of
personal efforts.

My candid advice is that you desist from sitting in mediocrity which is
the dark room of ignorance but rather give all you have and all it takes
to attain the fulfilment of your business vision. A great man said
"there is no mountain anywhere every man's mountain is his own
ignorance."

Therefore, study, study, study – do a lot of reading to learn the lingo
of event planning. Read relevant literatures because a man of
knowledge increases strength. Sign up for classes, attend relevant
seminars, watch videos that are relevant to this business and enhance
your practical knowledge.

Learn management, learn new things each and every day; crave for
every useful nugget of information in the area of excellent public
relations, strong networking and budgeting. This is the best way to
improve on capacity building and increase capabilities.

Why not think of enrolling for relevant classes and workshops as you
read through this book? If there is none in your community, go out
of your locality. You are greatly enhancing yourself by paying to get
your mind on proper footing. Never resist the advances of today's

technology for any reason this is why the ability to use the computer is also very important in this important.

You may have to use event planning software to perform work duties for each client. I have discovered that self - development is basically for best results. I will sincerely advice you do absolutely whatever it takes to get some experience. Inefficiency is inevitable without self - development.   None is ever too old to learn new things neither is your long years organizing event as an amateur, can be overlooked. Buy the truth and sell it not.

Experience is important but training is a must for success in this industry, it could be the single most important tool for event planners. Being able to constantly change your procedures comes only through relevant training. Oftentimes we need to stir up ourselves on things we think we already know. It encourages us to begin operating once again in powerful business principles that we have let slip away.

Training is an important aspect of development and it is essential in acquiring appropriate business acumen.   It enlightens and broadens our scope. At Movina Professional Managers we have trained not less than a hundred Event planners not decoration or catering but great resources that will upturn your business as an Event planner.

Most jobs are poorly executed by Event planners because of inadequate training. In this part of the globe, I will say with all humility that we assume to be experts in what we know little or nothing about. There is no true greatness in a man that is ignorant and yet shies away from personal development.

Expand your competence and ability on a regular basis and initiate personal learning process. As a matter of fact, continuous improvement is the watchword of great event planners. No matter your level attainment, learning should be seen as an essential tool for improved performance and excellence. Confidence in business is in your abilities and this can be developed through quality training.

When you lack confidence event planning becomes burdensome. For instance, how do you write winning proposals and boldly sell you products and service? That is why any area of inadequacy calls for your enhancement. What training does is to improve your strength and capabilities and eliminate weakness. Businesses today are being bombarded with change; so be wise to make learning a top priority. Adequate training of human resource brings about more responsible, ethical and sustainable businesses.

The trained professional planner is a coach, a mentor and counsellor to clients, employees and stakeholders but you see, you can't give what you don't have. This is not debatable, because everyone knows when you know where you are going you know when you will get there. The issue here is there is a common fad where some go into businesses, they know little or nothing about only because they have money but such people lack the technical knowhow. They invariably want to outshine other businesses when they can actually humble themselves to learn under those that know more than they do. There is nothing as paying as humility in learning. Be broad minded and never assume knowledge. I will say here that humility is required to learn under those who know more than you do. We can put off the ITK (I too know) syndrome and be equipped by getting trained.

In 2003, I needed to have ideas on event design and wedding styling which is an aspect of Event planning, at that time I already had my Master's degree so I registered with one of the big-time decorating firms then only for the owner at that time to be relocating out of the city where I reside but I had to humble myself to be tutored by young school levers who the firm was handed over to.

Our natural abilities need reinforcement which in all sense shows how well one can implement ideas better and faster. Learning is dynamic; you can't grow beyond the level of what you know. You must be more than just someone who is knowledgeable about the field but versatile and a proficient professional. Never shirk away from continuous training as training is always ongoing and upgrading. Do not let the grass grow under your feet.

Chapter Four

Achieving business success

Acquiring relevant skills in event planning constitute the only job security. People who are continually learning and upgrading their skills increase their value. Different event tasks are involved in Event planning and this has made it mandatory for you to have basic skills. Skills bring success this I believe is connected to the fact that people's lives depend on how skilled they really are. Skill is the ability to do something with ease and accuracy. Skills are developed by experience and continuous practice.

However good you are today your knowledge and skills are becoming obsolete very quickly. Event planning requires multidimensional skills and an eye for details. That is why you must improve on your skills for better performance. Skill and competence are far more important than friendly feeling. You must have a broad range of skills because of the different job tasks involved in event projects.

Do what others are doing and you will get the same result but do something different and you put them on guard. There are a number of tools and techniques that can be used to improve your skills. We are looking into just a few of it in this session having shown that skills can be learned and developed. If you lack any of the following skills, training will be appropriate.

Human resource management

Human resource management is the part of management function concerned with the maintenance of human relationships in an organization; and ensuring the well-being of employees, so they are given the best conditions in which to maximize their contribution to the business. Ensuring an event is adequately staffed with the right people, who are appropriately trained and motivated to meet its objectives, is fundamental to the event management process. Many events companies have an organizational structure that grows in terms of personnel as the event approaches, but quickly contract when it ends. From the human resources perspective, this creates a number of challenges, including working to short timelines to hire and select staff, and to develop and implement staff training, and needing to shed staff quickly.

Human resource management is all about but not limited to the following and has much more strategic function:

1. Recruitment
2. Selection
3. Welfare
4. Training/Development
5. Remuneration
6. Job specification

The main aspect of the human resource function for event companies include: recruitment and selection of staff and volunteers; training and development; wages and salary administration; and safety and welfare.

Training schemes for the staff must be initiated and developed by the company to ensure that each new member of staff undergoes an induction, and existing staff are trained as the need arises. Outside the actual company staff are contractors who are part-time workers who are skilled in various job options and are often cheaper to hire; and can be more flexible; then volunteers who often make up the bulk of people involved in delivering an event. In some instances, events are run entirely by volunteers.

The challenges presented by volunteers are many, and relate to matters such as volunteer sourcing, quality control, supervision, training and motivation.

There are several advantages of outsourcing work to independent contractors:

a. Your business has to pay for what it gets
b. Long term relationships can be built between you company and the contractor

c.   The contractor is negotiable on rates of pay or fees, especially when you know you have to compete with others for the same contractors. This is a common phenomenon in this business.

d.   Contracts can be written precisely to reflect needs and can include clauses to invoke time or quality penalties.

Employees should be assisted with personal problems, whether domestic or work; and adequate health and safety precautions and welfare services should be developed including hygiene matters relating to events.

Managing people is a basic necessity in event planning industry otherwise your actions, utterances and behaviour can pack up the business. There is no continuity in business without adequate knowledge of human resources whether in the area of relating to customers, employees, or competitors. There must be requisite knowledge of human relations and managing group behaviour. This is because good relations bring about high productivity.

Effective leadership

A leader is one whose productivity is in part, determined by others. Leadership is a function of designated position, but a title and position do not guarantee performance and productivity. In my work as a "coach," the most common question I get to ask is "how can I improve my performance so that I can earn more money." One can only build performance on strength. As an entrepreneur, your role is to shape the enterprise according to your vision and cultivate a team of capable people who are equipped and empowered to operate the business from day to day, independent from you. A leader knows the way shows the way and goes the way by being and he does this through performance. Leaders are proactive, and they seek and act on feedback.

Our leadership qualities should be able to influence people to willingly strive toward the achievement of group goals because we are in the peoples' business. When you know who you are, what you want and how to go about doing it right, then others will be inspired to follow you all the way. In other words, it is the willingness of others to follow that makes you a leader. Leadership skills necessary for event planners revolve around planning, preparation, willingness to try something new, and confidence to take risk.

What we need in this industry are planners at every level who can energize, excite and inspire their employees to do the things they don't necessarily like to do, but they do them and enjoy them.

Event planners that:

1. Focus on strategic issues
2. Doesn't hope for convenience
3. Involve everyone and welcome great ideas from everywhere
4. Do the right things
5. Can be trusted
6. Are Innovative

It will be difficult leading a team in a career you know nothing about. The ability to look at things objectively and understand things from different point of views make you an effective leader.

You must understand that the reason clients are hiring you is because you can help them get the big picture and actualize their vision and that you are active and not passive.

Event planners should be high motivators that take the lead in promoting their services, participating in event marketing, dining with influential media and politicians and also engage in seminar presentations. They should be able to have the three basic qualities that make a visionary leader effective. These are:

a. A good communicator
b. Ability to extend their vision to vendors and support staff
c. Ability to pitch in to help.

However, an event planner as the case may be must be more than someone who is simply very knowledgeable about a particular field but who has knowledge and insight of all immediate operations under his control this include but not limited to fashion, trends, staging and makeup.

Event planning is quite interesting if you possess the ability to influence people towards goal accomplishment. You need to influence your workforce to get the job done. This skill can best be developed by taking on leadership positions, volunteering and further enhancement through education and experience. If you don't develop yourself in the area of leading competently and managing things, you will never find it easy running your own business.

Effective communication

Communication is one of the basic functions of management in any organization and its importance can hardly be overemphasized. It is a process of transmitting information, ideas, thoughts, and opinions and plans between various parts of an organization. It is not possible to have human relations without communication. However, good and effective communication is required not only for good human relations but also for good and successful business.

The ability to communicate is a must have skill to event planners because is important to your success if you must work with others. The process of communication is transmission of ideas, information, opinions, comprehension and reaction. The reaction determines the sales. During a conversation, both parties need to clearly understand what is being communicated, especially when planning the details of an event. Analysing what you hear and asking questions clarifies what you have heard and encourages the speaker to expand on what she/he was saying. Active listening helps prevent misunderstanding when meeting with a client this means you must learn to paraphrase what the client has said. In business you continuously shift back and forth between the roles of the encoder and decoder.

Always concentrate on what the speaker is saying and practice not thinking about what you are going to say as soon as you get your chance. Rapid communication is key to customer excellence. Lack of communication is the explanation for every problem in an organization. Poor communication can only lead to wastage of time and may even hamper the progress of the event. How you speak to your clients as well as other stakeholders will best define your communication skills. So much success is realized from your ability to relate the needs of your clients to service providers. We should not forget telephone etiquette as well, which are an important aspect of good communication.

I read of a patient who went to visit a doctor, at the end of the investigation the doctor found the patient's problem to be his weight. He then advised the patient to go 10km every day and report back to him in seven days. On the 7th day he called the doctor and said he has lost weight but the only problem that needed to be sorted out is his being 70km away from the doctor. How well do you communicate?

Facing communication problem is quite common during event planning. Words mean different things to different people. The meaning of words is not in the words; they are in us. The point is that while you and I speak a common language –English, our usage of that language is far from uniform. There is a difference between hearing and listening. To hear is to pick up sound vibrations. Listening is making sense out of what we hear. To listen requires you pay attention, interpret and remember sound stimuli.

It then implies that to be an effective communicator in this field, you should be highly articulated, possessing solid listening skills that will enable you communicate skilfully for persuasive, informative and simulative purposes. Otherwise, it will be difficult getting all the little details involved in executing your job.

You will also need superior listening skill to read between lines when negotiating for jobs and this call for experience, patience and possessing the real fundamentals of finding the best in every person you are in contact with.

Reasons for effective communication

- For increased productivity: Communication enhances good human relation and encourages idea development and suggestions.
- For motivation and employee morale: Communication is a tool for motivation, which can improve morale of employees in your business. Conflict arises when there is ineffective communication between vendors, planners and clients.

Rapid communication is vital to customer excellence. It is only through effective communication you will get to know your customers and employees. Say less than necessary – when trying to impress people with words, the more you say, the more common you appear and the less in control. The more you say, the more likely you are to say something foolish. Talk 20% of the time and listen 80% of the time when making the deal.

According to Leonarda da Vinci (1945- 1519) "the oyster opens completely when the moon is full; and when the crab sees one, it throws a piece of stone or seaweed into it and the oyster cannot close again so that it serves the crab for meat. Such is the fate of him who opens his mouth too much and thereby puts himself at the mercy of the listeners". Be vast in differentiating between hearing and listening. Hearing is merely picking up sound vibrations while listening is making sense out of what you hear. This implies that listening requires paying attention, interpreting and remembering sound stimuli. Avoid interrupting the client during negotiations and all through execution stages. Let the person complete his or thought before you try to respond. Do not try to second guess peoples' thoughts. Most of us would rather speak our own ideas than listen to what someone else says. You cannot talk and listen at the same time.

It is very good to paraphrase that means you restate what the client has said in your own words. Rephrasing is an excellent control device to check on whether you are listening carefully and it's a control for verifying accuracy of your understanding.

Good communication leads to better team work and better understanding. This is because communication will be part of your daily job. In other words, effective communication will lead to better efficiency and relationship building. It as well enables you to create successful and memorable events that are used for specific effects.

To put off communication barriers:

1. Improve on listening skills
2. ii.   Read body language and facial expressions
3. iii.   Influence your team to improve performance
4. iv.   Overcome any language barrier
5. v.   Deal with conflict when it arises

People management

At its core Event planning is about relationship, relationship with clients, suppliers, stakeholders and company staff. The ability to establish and maintain those relationships is very important to your success. Winning a customer for the first time is arduous and often tedious. But you can win their loyalty by having pre-requisite people skills and meeting their demand – whether corporate or individual clients.

Dealing with people is probably the biggest problem you face, especially if you work in this industry. The man who has technical knowledge plus the ability to express his ideas, to assume leadership, and to arouse enthusiasm among men – that man is headed for higher earning power. The ability to relate with people is as purchasable a product as coffee or sugar. You should be willing to pay more for that ability than for any other under the sun. It is vital to know how to understand and get along with people; how to make people like you; and how to win others to your way of thinking.

Criticism and condemnation will never run any business but kindness, word of appreciation, and encouragement will inspire your organization with loyalty, enthusiasm and spirit of teamwork. The only way you can get anyone to do business with you is to give what they want. The deepest urge in human nature is the desire to be important. The desire for a feeling of importance is what makes the richest man in your town build a house far too large for his requirement.

This desire makes you want to wear the latest styles, drive the latest car, and talk about your business.

Sincere appreciation was one of the secrets of Rockefeller's success in handling men. We need to know how to nourish the self-esteem of our employees as we do our bodies by giving them kind words of appreciation that would sing in their memories for years like the music of the morning stars. This means, cultivating good relationship with employees and others will make them accessible to you.

Think about the benefits of your business to others. In other words, what can you do to help people? We need to learn to bait the hook to suit the fish. The only way to get the other fellow is to talk about what he wants and show him how to get it. Harmony in human relationship cannot be overemphasized. There can be no richer man than he who has found a labour of love and who is busily engaged in performing it. The first piece of advice for planners is first arousing in the other person an eager want. Before you persuade someone to do business with you pause and ask: How can I make him want to buy from me?

The secret of success lies in the ability to get the other person's point of view and see things from his angle as well as from your own.

Every business owner is first a salesman and thousands of salesmen are pounding the pavement today, tired, discouraged and underpaid. Why? They are always thinking only of what they want. If a salesman can show us how his services will help solve our problems he won't need to sell us, we'll buy.

Strategic interpersonal behaviour shape or influence impressions formed by an audience about you and your business. Your business conduct whether positive or negative will affect your rating by your clientele.

a. Be simple in your language, no staff or client enjoy being harassed.
b. Read people to serve them better and communicate more frequently.

The answer to uncertainty and anxiety in business is good interpersonal relationship and personal management standard, this includes managing time and stress alongside with staying organized.

It is very mandatory to appear cheerful, assured and poised at all times in addition to being positive, forceful and decisive. Knowing your clients personally is a good way to building trust.

Creativity

Creativity is part of our design as humans. Our uniqueness which is borne out of creativity sets us apart in business.

Event planning and management business provides an ample opportunity for planners to exhibit their creative skills, this means taking your client's vision and amplifying it with creatively to deliver an exceptional event. Creativity means coming up with unique ideas that is thinking outside the box and making new synergistic connections. It is the ability to see beyond the ordinary and create what does not exist. You should think out multiple solutions to problems rather than settling for just one; in which case you give yourself permission to be playful, inquisitive, flexible and versatile. Often is just lack of imagination that keeps a person from his potential.

Having the prerequisite creative flair means coming up with innovative ideas and turning such ideas into value for the event, thus creating profitable business activities. Creativity is never ending; it is a continuous activity for an event planner, always seeing new ways of doing things with little concern for how difficult they might seem. Thinking of new ideas is like shaving, if you don't do it daily, you're a bum.

Creativity skill is relevant for event design. It is not for a talented few but for everyone humble enough to learn how to effectively put things in their proper perspective. There is need for determination, enthusiasm and persistence, because some clients come to you with little or no ideas at all of how they would like their event to look. You must have reasons why you can do things, the way clients want it and why you will do it differently. The important thing is not to stop asking questions. Never lose a holy curiosity.

To discover how easily ideas for creativity comes, open your mind and think on all old approaches to doing things and then find out new ways of doing such things differently to get better results. Ideas for creativity can be generated from inspiration sources such as magazines, newspapers, television as well as everywhere else. Watch your competition and develop new concepts from their actions and experiences but never imitate them to the point of copying out-rightly.

Constantly frustrate old business traditions with creativity and imagination.

Experiment on new strategies that will set the standard for your business. It will greatly interest you to know that the reason clients hunt for event planners is for their creative abilities. There is nothing as important as being able to come up with fresh ideas which they cannot find anywhere. The truth is that good ideas bring good money, when you have the relevant idea; you have a terrific in flock to your business. Put your mind to work regularly and try attending events, time permitting, is only by going to such places you understand the guest's perspective which is important to satisfying your clients. When crisis is envisioned, you will need to use your creativity. It means there are times you may adopt creative problem-solving ability to quickly come up with alternative arrangements.

Always approach every event from different perspectives; you cannot afford to be stereotyped in business. Ability to initiate changes to existing rules makes a star. Clients want to see uniqueness in their events in which case you can't do without being current with the happenings around your community.

Everyday life has something new to offer, if you focus very well you will find inspiration in all things.

To be a creative event planner, consider the following:

    a.   Constant practice is the ultimate action step
    b.   Ask searching questions from clients, staff and suppliers
    c.   Think outside of the box. Meditation heightens creativity. It is a most valuable tool that ensures you are at your best every day.

Enhancing creativity is the business of event planning. The bottom line is for you to be current, and trendy since creativity and originality are of utmost importance.

Chapter Five

The event planning formula

The "official definition" as released by United State Department of Labor "says event planning consists of coordinating every detail of meetings and conventions, from the speakers and meeting location to arranging printed materials and audio – visual equipment." This will be irrelevant without been able to execute plans; this is actually the management phase of any event.

You wouldn't think of being at the top without having projections, making plans, checking the plans over, evaluating and re-evaluating those plans and lastly sticking to the plans. A wise man said "goal setting is the first step to overt, positive action. Goals are a track to run on, a course to take. They are not substitute to reality." What you want to achieve is the goal, how you achieve it is the activity. Suppose a man is about building a tower, will he not first sit down and estimate the cost to see if he has enough money to complete?

You will juggle post its, phone numbers, booking the perfect speakers and endless lists to make the most spectacular of shindigs (a lively party), entertainment, getting ideas on dream venues with the perfect décor and sorting everything from the wait staff to the evaluation. Put simply you will apply top notch project management skills to the creation and development of events.

It takes ten years to win gold at the Olympics, according to the head coach of ROWSA, Roger Barrow. Indeed, there is no substitute for meticulous planning.

Planning involves a lot of thinking through ideas, studying and proper arrangement of necessary details to achieve desired goals. A wise man said "proper prior planning prevents poor performance."

Effective planning depends upon response to environmental factors that revolve round the community, in which the organization is operating, the personalities of the group members, cultural influence as well as the time required for decision making. In as much as long – range planning is extremely important in this industry {such as booking ahead of time for specific events}, proper planning to achieve your set goal is vital. Taking into account the situation in its entirety and designing an environment for business performance is a relevant aspect of the planning process. Because of the unique nature of each special event, special planning is a process that must continuously occur from the start of the bid until the end of the event

You can't effectively plan without setting goals and coming up with a design of action plan in the future. Planning events answers ahead to the issues of what you need do, why you should do it, where you want it done and when to do it. Planning well ahead helps you Identify specific problems, and also gives you adequate knowledge of who you want to involve and make suggestions where necessary. It is always advisable to spend minimum amount of time in planning and be on the hot line of activity.

You may need to consider the following issues when planning your event:

- Event on highway
- Outdoor Sites and permit
- Staging and structures
- Risk Management
- Food hygiene
- Water
- Emergency lighting
- Inflatable
- Stalls
- Installation and Equipment
- Toilets
- Emergency Evacuation
- Community Safety
- Environmental issues
- Site Plan

- Disabled Assess
- Overcrowding
- Crowd dynamics
- Bomb Threat
- Fire fighting
- First Aid
- Information point
- Public address system
- Staff safety

Benefits of planning

- It enables planners to detect and solve problems
- Alternative strategies are highlighted for consideration
- Staff responsibilities are classified
- Uncertainty about the event is reduced.

Because of the unique nature of each event, planning must continuously occur from start of the bid until the end of the event.

The event planning process is guided by what the client wants to achieve, which helps the event company develop a creative direction and structure that begin with the initial planning and culminate with the post event follow-up. The event profession focuses on the rationale or goal of having an event, and whether it is achieved.

Knowing who an event planner is, sets precedence for what we will discuss in this chapter.

Briefly, let me say that the plans you make are like the power of life. Event planning is organizing professionally focused events for a particular target audience. This could be corporate as well as private events. Planning events has to do with planner's ability to define goals, establish strategy and develop plans to coordinate tasks. There are six Ps to an effective event namely: Purpose, Program, People, Place, Pennies and Promotion. All of these determine the success of the event.

Every event needs a beginning. When meeting with a client for the first time, you will need to gather some preliminary information before you can showcase your ideas. This interview will become very important later for your proposal and presentations. You will need to take excellent notes. After meeting with the client, preparation should be done for your next meeting. Usually the first question asked - the reason for the occasion. This sets the tone for the rest of the interview.

There is a chance you have spoken at length about the occasion in your initial phone conversation with the client. If this is the case be sure to revisit the detail with the client during your meeting. Hold onto your trade secrets until after she has signed a contract. Proper steps should be taken to protect new products, services and operational techniques, it will be extremely difficult to maintain and expand the company's share of the market because others will be free to copy these ideas as if they were their own. Misappropriation refers to the wrongful taking of your trade secrets by those who had a duty not to take or use this information for their own competitive advantages.

If you are shopping venues for your client, be sure her event needs, matches the capacity and style of the venue.

Event survey

Success is an indispensable tool when planning events be it seminars, workshops, retreats, tradeshows or exhibitions to mention a few. Survey enables you to gauge expectations, understand participant's reaction during the event, gather and analyse information and measure effectiveness of your message long after the event is over.

There are rules that contribute to event success when carrying out survey:

- Ask your audience what they want before the event. What is their expectation from the event? Knowing this will help you provide the content that best appeals to their needs. Far too often event planners focus on what they want to say rather than what the audience wants to know. If you were buying a

set of settees you would research on your interest and make
your decision based upon the factors that are important to
you. You need to determine their needs and what is
important to them. It helps to create program that is of
value to attendees. Do the participants prefer morning,
afternoon or evening event? How far is she willing to travel
to an event? Which of the topics interest her most? Measure
your marketing efforts? Ask how attendees heard about your
event.

- Keep attendees engaged during the event. Once the event is
  underway you need to create a level of excitement and
  interest among attendees. One way to keep attendees
  involved and interested during the event is to have them
  complete a survey form and then share the result with them
  at the wrap off of the event.

- Ask attendees for their feedback on the event. Receiving
  feedback on event is critical in determining whether it was
  successful or not. Conduct a post event survey and ask the
  audience what they thought about the overall event, the
  content, the speakers, and the facilities. Determine logistical
  success or failures.

Keep the information line open with your event audience by finding
out what they need encouraging their participation and gathering their
feedback. We shall discuss on this in a later chapter.

Event creation

It is also important to have a knowledge of great steps to creating
successful event, this will enable us establish priorities. These are the
why, what, where, when, who and how of any event planning. It
mustn't necessarily follow this sequence. See figure 5.1.

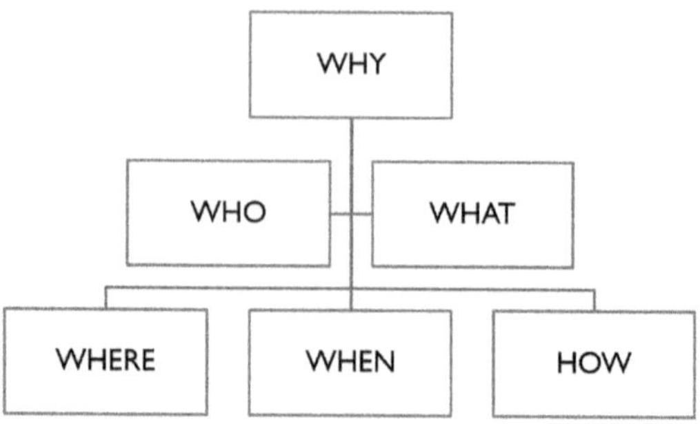

Figure 5.1: Creating a successful event

WHY: Why are you intending to do the event? Are you doing it for commercial profit, to increase business revenue, promotion of culture or is it for charity? It might be a celebration such as the country's centenary or political reason? It might be to promote a city's image or to attract visitors. Did you have permission of the parent organization to organize an event in their name? Knowing the purpose for the event, the problem to be solved or the opportunity to be pursued is important for every event project. The purpose for which an event is organized is crucial value. Clarity of purpose is important in event planning business.

It is of no use knowing the purpose and not effectively pursuing it precept upon precept to its actualization. Someone says when purpose is not known abuse is inevitable.

WHAT: What concept will best serve the purposes of the event? In situations where concept has not been identified brainstorming is encouraged.

This brings the strategic intent, the goals and objectives of the event to clarity. What are you intending to do? Will it be leisure or a sporting event? People can come up with ideas and some of these can be blended or combined and the best ideas selected after been refined to create the event concept. This event concept is developed as a theme and applied to many different aspects of the event as possible. Make sure the purpose for the event is important enough to merit the time and expense needed to properly stage, publicize and evaluate the event. Having clear objectives would help you set the tone for team members. Being able to set objectives alone doesn't make someone a good event planner just as ability to tie small knot in confined space does not make a person a surgeon. But without the ability to set objectives, it is not possible to be an adequate planner.

WHERE: This has to do with both the internal and external environment. Where are you intending to do it? Where is the best place to stage the event? Where do you want the event to take place? Is the location worth it?

The venue should both accommodate the needs of the event as well as give it a unique character and atmosphere.

Will it be on a private land, town hall or conference centre? Will you be able to get the necessary permission from the land owner? Other vital issues to consider will include availability, security, cost, transport, parking and facilities.

WHEN: This addresses the milestone event and timing. Everything revolves around the date of your special event. When are you intending to do it? Ideally you want to have three potential dates in mind so that you can compare availability and prices across the board. Try to include different days of the week for maximum flexibility. Know when the event is scheduled to take place in terms of date and time of the day and season. Is it during the rains? Is the weather right for an outdoor event? Will it be a festive period or holidays? Will the event hold in the morning, afternoon, or evening? What is happening on that day such as other events? Even a single hour difference can make an impact on your planning, so you really need to get specific about your anticipated time frames.

Know the target market, the type of event – indoor or outdoor, these are strong determining factors.

WHO: This comprises of the sponsors, vendors, the planner, the team members and guests to be invited. Target the group that have special stake in the event.

Who do we want to attend the event? Is the event targeted at local residents and / or visitors? The event might be educational, or a more general audience. It is important to know the target as this will drive the marketing and promotion of the event.

HOW: This reflects on how the event will be executed. How are you intending to do it? Have you got a plan of exactly what it is you intend to do? How much should you charge for attendance? Will you call on sponsors to help offset costs? What will exhibitors pay to participate? All the little details should be noted in its entirety by staying organized. An athlete who runs in a race cannot win the prize unless he obeys the rule.

Generally, an event is not just party planning. This is the case whether you are considering a path with social events or corporate. This could be as simple as:

- Starting to plan at least six months, and in many cases, a year ahead of time.
- Talking with other planners who have successfully staged similar events.

These aforementioned stages of event planning are very important and are dependent on the type of event, and logistics associated with it. Knowing well that the reason you are been hired is for your organizing abilities means you can always bring out the best in you per time if that is your desire. Can you imagine a soldier on active service who wants to please his commanding officer getting mixed up with irrelevant issues? Similarly, the planner must not engage in task that will not bring about success. The bottom line here is focus on acquiring knowledge.

Theming

A theme is a common idea that runs through the entire event. The theme of an event differentiates it from other events. Thinking outside the box has become a bit cliché and yet it is immensely important in event planning. Is it going to be a theme to the event? Planning event themes that coordinate all aspect of the event is an essential part of a successful and memorable occasion. Whatever the nature of the event, once the theme is established, the elements of the event must be designed to fit in with the theme.

From small details such as souvenirs and text font on invitation to large details such as table displays, catering and stage management must be done to harmonize the event theme. It could be something elaborate like a costume theme, party theme, historic or movie theme or something more relevant to the company, based on a new product launch. Take an orange theme for example; you could arrange various shades of orange, orange balloons, table arrangements, fizzy bubble machines and orange desserts. Unique gifts and favours can be designed with company logo and name to accompany event.

For a company retreat at a beach side mansion you could suggest a clambake for the menu holding in august. Because the event is happening in August, offer a light white wine and a bucket of different drinks. You have to be creative for that touch and innovative style needed to make your event truly memorable.

Clients will sometimes choose a theme based on music, colour or cuisine. For an annual gala fundraiser, a black- and-white ball in which all of the guests are asked to dress in formal attire is an example of a colour themed event. A theme based on cuisine might be a Chinese or Mexican fiesta that features a mariachi band. The elements of staging revolve around the theme.

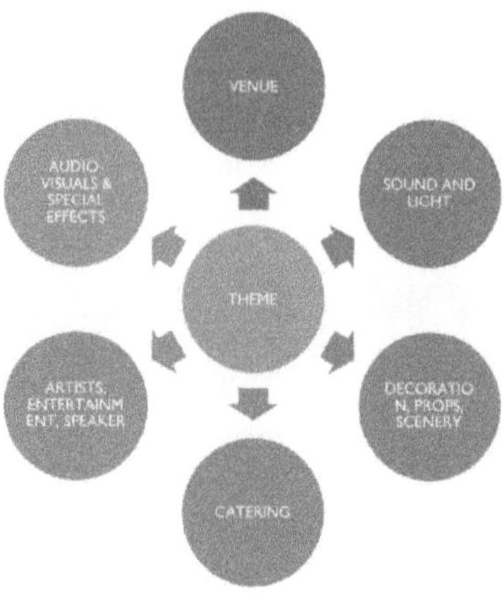

Figure 5.2: Theme management quadrant

Source: Event Management by Glenn Bowdin et al (2006).

When you sit with a client for the initial interview, ask him if he has any ideas for theme. It is likely that he will have a theme in mind and will ask you to expand on it. What event managers should always ask their clients is what they want to achieve. You may see themes on invitations, in magazines, or hear about them, these you need to keep in a log book or notebook as a new Event planner. This can be replaced with a scrapbook of your events complete with photos once you have gained experience.

Chapter Six

Successful event strategy

Business activities for an event planner include planning, production, marketing, design and conceptualization, budgeting, risk management, logistics, human resources, staging, and evaluation. Each of the areas continuously affect each other over the event life cycle. No strategic plan and no scheme for strategy implementation can foresee all events and problems that will arise. Making adjustments and mid-course corrections is a normal and necessary part of strategic management. When responding to new conditions involving either the strategy or its implementation, prompt action is often needed. In a crisis, the typical approach is to push key subordinates to gather information and formulate recommendations, personally preside over extended discussions of the proposed responses, and try to build a quick consensus among members of the executive inner circle. When time permits a full-fledged evaluation is necessary.

The approach involves the following:

- Staying flexible and keeping a number of options open
- Asking a lot of questions
- Gaining in-depth information from specialists
- Encouraging subordinates to participate in developing alternatives and proposing solutions.
- Getting the reactions of many different people to proposed solutions to test their potential and political acceptability
- Seeking to build commitment to a response by gradually moving toward a consensus solution.
- Strategy leaders should be proactive as well as reactive in reshaping strategy and how it is implemented.

People fail in business not only because they don't plan but they also know little or nothing about proper management procedures. Developing a strategy is the most creative task you will ever undertake because planning is crucial to event managers but importantly is implementing the strategy.

As mentioned, event management companies service a variety of areas including corporate events like product launches, television-based events like competitions, special events like concerts, award nights, film premieres and music releases, star nights and fashion shows, corporate seminars and conferences, retail marketing programs including road shows: training programs, event promotions and private shows like weddings and parties.   The event manager should be an expert at creative, technical and logistical procedures.

Strategic concept

Event planning and management is predominantly about creating an experience. Bear in mind that first impression last. It is important when embarking on any event regardless of its scale to take the correct approach and use the right techniques and strategy to ensure that your event is successful and you're also able to thrive in face of competition.

Crafting business strategy that yields sustainable competitive advantage (SCA) has three facets:

- Developing where your company has the best chance to win competitive edge
- Developing products or service attributes that have strong buyer appeal and set the company apart from rivals, and
- Neutralizing the competitive moves of rival company

Strategy is a procedure, tasks, styles, the order in which business ought to be done. There are strategies to employ in every business.

Top event planning companies are "customer oriented." They have a clear sense of their target customers and their needs and also have plan of actions intended to accomplish specific goals. They have developed a distinctive strategy for satisfying those needs.

Strategy is the creation of a unique and valuable position involving a different set of activities. It is a unified, comprehensive integrated plan, relating the advantages of the firm to the challenges of the environment. To buttress further, a company that is strategically positioned "performs different activities from rivals or performs similar activities in different ways." Simply put, it is carrying out a project plan in skilful ways.

Many companies believe that they can establish a long-lasting competitive advantage by performing similar activities better than their competitors. But today competitors can rapidly copy the operationally effective company using benchmarking and other tools thus tapering the advantage of operationally effectiveness.

This career path is considered as one of the strategic marketing and communication tools used by establishment of all sizes in the business world.

You can service a variety of clients and their events including corporate events, retail marketing programs, event promotions, and television-based events, special events and private shows.

Planners must adapt a strategy for achieving its goals, consisting of a marketing strategy, and a compatible technology and sourcing strategy. See figure 6.1.

Figure 6.1 Strategy formulation

A lot of people get into this business without a true understanding of the basics needed to be successful in it. Research is required to gather the basics before venturing into any business.   Wining in this business takes knowledge, experience, creativity and efficient service that generate good results.

Some of the basic strategies to employ include but not only the following:

- A mission statement that will specify the purpose of the event, the scope of the business, values and philosophy that guide the event.
- Financial and strategic objectives
- Craft a strategy to achieve performances
- Implement strategy
- The strategic management

A company that is strategically positioned "performs different activities from rivals or performs similar activities in different ways."

You should adapt a strategy for achieving goals, consisting of a marketing strategy and a compatible technology and sourcing strategy. Many event planning businesses are small and do not use formal management or marketing techniques. One of our key priorities should be to increase customer volume and revenues by making our businesses more market oriented.

<u>Swot analysis in event planning</u>

This is a major tool in understanding the premix of event planning. It is an extremely useful tool for understanding and decision making for all sorts of situations in business and organizations.

It offers professional event planners an effective evaluative technique that aids decision making process. The SWOT analysis is used for business planning, strategic planning, competitor evaluation, marketing, business and product development and research reports.

The acronym SWOT is a strategic planning tool for evaluating Strength, Weaknesses, Opportunity and Threat. Strength and Weaknesses are regarded as distinctly as internal factors, whereas Opportunities and Threats are regarded distinctly as external factors.

SWOT is a very flexible tool. SWOT can be used to assess the following:

- A business decision
- A company (its position in the market, commercial viability etc.)
- A potential partnership
- A strategic option such as entering a new market
- Outsourcing a service, activity or resource
- Personal financing planning
- Project planning and Project management
- Education and qualifications planning and decision making.

Whatever the application, be sure to describe the subject (or purpose or question) for SWOT analysis clearly so you remain focused on the central issue.

Assuming you are organizing a corporate event, it is necessary for you as an event planner to do research of the products/services promoted and sold by your corporate client. Then analyse the following based on available information.

- What is the market value and market share of the company and its products?
- Find out how the company promotes its products
- Who are the customers of the products?
- How does the company want to build/enhance the image associated with the product also known as brand image?
- What are the features of the products?
- What are the advantages and disadvantages of the product in comparison to competitors' products?

The result of this research will later help in making effective promotional campaign for corporate events.

SWOT analysis is a strategic planning tool which is used to identify and analyse the strength, weakness, opportunity and threat involved in your project. SWOT analysis can also be done in your organization. It is one of the most used tools to understand the context in which we are organizing our event. We need to come up with a strategy that leverages on our strengths to exploit opportunities or defend us from threats. We should also be aware of our weaknesses to find new resources or to protect them from risks. SWOT analysis will provide a detailed snapshot (synopsis) of a company's health. You can always think of this tool to diagnose and fix what's a bit worn, what's on the verge of breaking down or what is already broken and needs replacement.

This tool also offers professional event planners an effective evaluative technique to aid the decision-making process. See figure 6.2.

STRENGTH

- Advantages of proposition?
- Capabilities
- Competitive Advantages?
- Experience, Knowledge, data?
- Price, value, quality?
- Cultural, attitudinal, behavioural?

WEAKNESSES

- Disadvantages of proposition?
- Gaps in capabilities?
- Lack of competitive strength?
- Own known vulnerabilities?
- Reliability of data, plan predictability?
- Process and systems?

OPPORTUNITIES

- Market development?
- Competitor's vulnerability?
- Industry or lifestyle trends
- Technology development and innovation?
- New markets, vertical, horizontal?
- Niche target market?
- Major contracts, tenders?

THREATS

- Political effects?
- Legislative effects?
- Environmental effects?
- I.T developments?
- Market demand?
- New technologies, services, ideas?
- Employment market?

Your professional strength

Brainstorm a bit; make a list of your personal, professional and educational strength. Be as detailed as possible, write it down and get it printed out. The list can help you develop your marketing materials and may give you hype on those days when you need one.

1. Strong funding
2. Huge Profit Margin
3. Skilled manpower
4. Availability of financial resources
5. Quality service
6. Concentrate on your strengths
7. Work on improving on your strengths. Be updated in skills and knowledge and more importantly when it's no longer adequate.

8. Occasionally carry out a self- appraisal of your abilities, resources, interest and present situation and match up with mission statement.

Weakness

1. Weakness arises from areas where you lack sufficient training, expertise or experience that can outwit competition.
2. Poor market share
3. Poor promotional activity
4. Poor business communication
5. Less experience in the business
6. Less experience in the business

Opportunity

Event planners that are seen as market leaders can be vulnerable to a competitor who discovers a gap in the market place.

Opportunities may be derived from:

1. Friends or relations occupying strategic positions
2. Diversification into related area of interest
3. Improving business
4. Change in social environment

Threats

Threat comes with anything which affects the success of your business.

1. Increasing competition
2. Fighting during events
3. Unstable government regulations and policies

Develop on your weakness and build more on your strength. Areas that threaten the production of a successful event must of necessity be outsourced to professional vendors who have more proficiency than you do.

Remember an ignorant man stands at the midpoint of life; this is true to everything including business. What you knew yesterday is not enough for today. People have more choices today than ever, if you can't meet their need they will certainly look elsewhere.

Smart objectives for events

There is a quote by Yogi Berra, the zany former New York Yankee catcher "if you don't know where you are going, you will wind up somewhere else."

That's the reason you need a strategic plan. It is a roadmap to help you determine the direction in which you wish to go, and the specific goals you will need to accomplish to get there. A strategic plan starts with a stamen of core values, which may include things like client satisfaction, ethical business practices, staff satisfaction, training, and motivation; community service and operating an environmentally conscious business. From these core values, an event planner can develop a Mission statement – a succinct sentence that sums up the company's mission. After the mission statement, comes the Vision Statement – a concise summary where you want to be in the future.

Your mission and vision statement lead naturally to establish goals for the operation.

SMART is used when describing goals. An example of SMART goals might be increasing sales and profits by 30% each year for the next five years.

Specific　　　=　　　Goals to be accomplished must be easily understood, concise and unambiguous; clearly state what you want to achieve

Measurable　　　=　　　Measurable in statistical terms; is it easy to measure the objectives you set? There should be no question about whether one attains, or falls short of a goal. It may be measured in terms of quality, cost, quantity, or time.

Attainable   =   the goals must be just out of reach, but
they are not out of sight! The best goals challenges and motivates you
and your team. If it is practically impossible it may be too frustrating.

Relevant =   the goals must fit well with your long-term mission
and vision, your objectives, and the results you expect. It must be
relevant to the resources available; can you really achieve them with the
current resources you have?

Time-bound   =   There must be a specific deadline for
completion of each goal.

Once you set goals there must be certain trade-offs. To increase sales
for instance may require raising prices, hiring more staff to be able to
complete tasks for the events, or spending money on advertising. The
major goals can be broken into smaller, intermediate steps, with a time
line to keep the company on track.

And remember, goals are not just for the business owner. The staff
and other professionals employed by the company suck as banker
should also be aware of the goals. Too often, Event planners believe
they can do everything themselves. They fail to ask for or accept
advice from outside consultants and colleagues. It is far more
intelligent to ask for assistance when you need it.

Finally, as soon as a goal is set, take some action on it.

The last part of the strategic management process is to re-evaluate
your mission, vision and goals periodically. Times changes, trends
change, and you become aware of new information.

<u>Vendor sourcing</u>

Event Planners have quite a number of service providers to help them
meet their objectives and most of these will certainly be out sourced.

To an Event planner a service provider is one that is directly involved
in the services that clients are in need of. In the field of Event
planning service providers also known as vendors are quite numerous
and in varied categories. But you need to remember that your

reputation is dependent on the success or failure of service providers. We find a situation where the Event planner is same as service provider of all or most services. This makes it difficult for the actual validity of tasks. It baffles me how on earth you can evaluate your service if you are the caterer, a disk jockey, a baker, a decorator, an equipment rental, a calligrapher and providing all services for same client at the same time?

Event planners rely on the expertise, professionalism and trust from service providers and suppliers to provide the best in services and products. Whereas the service provider looks to planners for proper guidance, concise logistics and fair and honest treatment the client looks to Event planners to put together a knowledgeable and hardworking team that will execute an outstanding function. The service providers are a prime source for networking as they meet with people every day who are looking for your service. In this career field, you wear out easily when you tend to do everything all alone; you need others who are efficient in various areas of event planning. I would advise you choose those who have a great reputation and great service delivery system in your community.

Work out an improved planner – service provider relationship that generates confidence and effectiveness.

A better understanding of this relationship will bring about a remarkable improvement in performance which has a direct positive impact. Most service providers expect you to negotiate creatively and many will give you discounts if is requested for. Be convinced of what you can do best and find great human resources to out-source the other tasks.

The appropriate service provider

These are a few examples of vendors whose service are valuable to Event planners:

1. AD specialty Companies
2. Audio/visual Companies, lighting and sound
3. Caterers

4. Party Supply Stores/Crafts
5. Disk Jockeys
6. Entertainment Brokers
7. Graphic Artists
8. Photographers
9. Printers
10. Rental Supply Stores
11. Decorators
12. Florists

Site selection

Where events are held is probably the single most important detail of any event. Researching and selecting the right venue for an event therefore is one of the foremost duties of an Event planner. The reason is that researching will help you to recommend great and sleek event sites that are not only attractive but spacious and secured for guests. The place is not all about chairs and tables but characteristic atmosphere, adequate and comfortable seating, space for entertainment, stages or dancing.

As soon as you have gotten possible dates for an event, you search for an appropriate space. You need to have the knowledge of all existing fun places within your locality that fit into a particular event.

a. Basics factors to consider include are:
b. The venue fee
c. The hall capacity
d. The refund policy if any
e. Cleanliness of the facility and cost of cleaning
f. Fee negotiation

The planner must find answers to the questions that pertain to the sites of the event. Some questions to consider include;

1. Has the proposed site been surveyed for inherent hazards by the nature of its location, and have any been identified?
2. Does the site have adequate access and staging area for large numbers of emergency vehicles in a major incident?

3. Is the site layout such that, in the event of a mass casualty situation, space is available for an on-site triage area to permit stability medical treatment prior to removal of critical patients?

4. Is such an area accessible to ambulances, to eliminate the need to carry patients' long distances?

5. Does the site allow for adequate crowd regulation such as flow barriers?

6. Have any legal permits required been applied for, and obtained, such as parade permit and fire safety permit?

7. Will public health authorities be available on site during the event to monitor public health compliance?

8. Will a first aid room, tent or vehicle be on site?

9. Will the site use regular police officers for onsite policing or will private security officers be engaged?

10. Have you put contingency plans in place?

Try selecting original locations and venues that are within reach and offer an all-inclusive solution. Always find out if there are restrictions as to the use of materials and equipment.

Logistics

Every good event project manager needs control skill for logistics. Logistics represent all the details that make the event happen and it covers:

- Supply Flows for event material, facilities and services
- Flow control of customers, products, and services during the event
- Information network during the event

Logistics refers to a group of related activities all in the movement and storage of products and information as it has to do with the task at hand. It is seen as a process of planning, implementing and controlling the efficient and effective flow of people and or goods and services for the purpose of conforming to client's or guests' requirement. Logistics management aims to develop and maintain the abilities to provide all needed support of special events.

Logistics is a collection of many functional activities through which the different factors and conditions (inputs) are converted into successful event output and outcome. These activities could be:

- Transportation
- Inventory maintenance
- Order Processing
- Supply, Procurement, Acquisition
- Purchasing
- Protective Packing
- Warehousing
- Storage and Handling
- Information, maintenance, and support activities.

Logistics management is the responsibility of the event planner. Therefore, planning any event is a logistical issue which is important to consider. That is, when it must be done and how it should be done. Poor logistics will ruin even the best event. The basic tasks necessary to do the job may include:

1. Decide goals and Theme
- Set a clear concise goal. Event must have a purpose and that purpose should ultimately contribute to the company's bottom line. Most events fail because a goal is not set and communicated.
- Themes make the event fun.
2. Research your audience
- Know who you will invite and why you are inviting them
- Who could your audience be?
- Invitations
3. Outline budget
   Take your different categories and assign estimates as well as administration cost.
4. Create event name and logo
5. Contact potential sponsors

6. Visit and select potential site
7. Diagram site
   Sketch a floor plan of the site
8. Make signs

What signs will you need?

- Choose evaluation methods
- Plan publicity campaign
- Select volunteers and form committees
- Contact media
- Select vendors and negotiate price
- Draft a menu
- Design registration
- Choose a serving style
- Shop for supplies
- Installation and set up
- Get ready for the day
  - On – site staff
  - On – site supervision
- Clean up and close up
- Meet for evaluation
- Appreciate everyone involved in making the event a success
- Write and file report

With many activities going on simultaneously; pre-event, at event and post event, I discovered there are many little details to take into cognizance. Major areas to consider and plan for include: marketing, size of space, entertainment, utility support needed, setup, coordination, cleanup, emergency plans and transportation.

Efficient logistical processes are used to create a sustainable competitive advantage this is done by designing a system which fulfils client's need better than competition. Due to the complexity of this business, a superior logistic system is a key asset that cannot be easily duplicated. It is used as an effective competitive weapon. The output of your logistic system is customer service and your duty is to design a system that delivers a desired level of client service at the lowest total cost.

Chapter Seven

The project management of events

The job of an event planner is similar to that of a project manager, meaning event planning focuses on event project management skills that are needed for running through a professional event and evaluating same. It then becomes suitable applying project management to the creation and development of ceremonies and functions.

The event planner creates program that address the purpose, message and impression that their organization is trying to communicate.

Depending on the event you are into, you are involved in creating event designs, budget management, staff coordination, marketing and public relations as well as applying project management techniques.

A project is a temporary endeavour with a defined beginning and end (usually time constrained and often constrained by funding or deliverables) undertaken to meet unique goals and objectives typically to bring about beneficial change or added value.

The primary challenge of project management is to achieve all of the project goals and objectives while recognizing the preconceived constraints. Typical constraints called triple constraints are scope, time and budget. The secondary challenge is to optimize the allocation of necessary inputs and integrate them to meet pre-defined objectives.

Project management has to do with application of knowledge, skills, tools and techniques to meet event project requirement. It involves the overall responsibility for the successful planning, execution, monitoring, control and closure of the project. See figure 7.1.

One of the many skills required of a project manager is the ability to ask searching questions and persevere until a clear answer is obtained.

The project management cycle

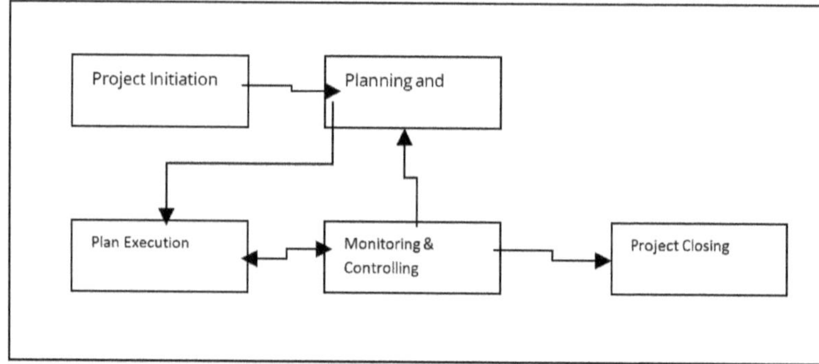

Figure 7.1: Project Management Cycle

In Project management, planning, organizing and management of the resources required to complete specific tasks are necessary skills. The planner must of necessity be prepared to effectively and simultaneously manage the four basic elements of a project: resources, scope, time, and money. All these elements are interrelated. She should be able to manage the resources assigned to the event, such human resources are service providers, employees, sponsors, volunteers. Managing event resources is more than managing people and part of managing resources means having the right people, with the right skills, and doing the right task. Maximum use of resources includes:

- Ensuring right men are recruited for right job
- Keeping materials at the right place
- Optimization of enterprise resources such as money, equipment, and people
- Continuity in business. This means activities must go on continuously without disruption of work.
- Success preceding every other thing.

The planner must also have the wherewithal to manage materials and equipment which depends on the nature of the project examples are banners, posters, audio visual aids, AP rigs, stage sound equipment, and lighting fixtures. It is mandatory to have the right equipment in the right place at the right time and have all necessary supplies it needs to operate properly.

The event planner creates programs that address the purpose message or impression that their organization or client is trying to communicate. Event planners work long and non-traditional hours to plan and execute all details related to a variety of meeting formats including seminars, conferences, tradeshows, executive retreats, incentive programs, golf events, convention and other programs.

The professional planner must of necessity determine what task to be done who does the task, how tasks are to be grouped, who reports to whom and where decisions are to be made. If you don't know where you are going you are sure losing focus. There is need for specificity in defining the goals of an event and getting through with the means by which such goals are achieved. It is your duty to ensure event is hazard free in the area of knowledge about various rules and regulations regarding events to safety and security issues. Successful planners must be vast in the following:

- Verbal and written communication
- Organization and time management
- Project management and multi-tasking
- Understand Microsoft office application
- Detail and deadline oriented
- Calm and personable under pressure
- Budget management
- Staff management
- Marketing and public relations
- Interpersonal skills with all levels of management

Successful event planners will have knowledge of the following:

- Venue selection
- Entertainment
- Catering
- Production
- Transportation

- Gifts and Souvenirs
- Lodging
- Conference services

Every project management thinks into the future. The better your plan, the better result attained. Sit down and imagine. Get the facts at all cost.

Imagine yourself as a person attending an event and ask the following questions:

- How did you get the information?
- When did you hear about the event?
- Why will you want to attend the event?
- How did you get people engaged?
- How will you evaluate the event?
- How much is good value?

Management fundamentals

The basic definition of management is effectively getting things done through people, that is, the enormous intellectual ability to get things done in a unique and precise format.

The management functions of an event planner include but not limited to planning and research, organization and coordinating, human resources, financial and physical resources, budgeting, controls risk management, marketing and communication, impact and performance evaluation.

Professional management may be competent, responsive and performing. In management, there is need to separate resources, capital, crucial physical resources, time and knowledge. But what matters in the end is the total overall productivity of a specific institution in using the resources. What matters is the total overall productivity of this event business.

To most of us, "deadline" is a scary word, but not to professionals. All projects have due dates when the event is completed and this must be carried out to the later. Meeting deadlines, making personal visits, making phone calls are major issues to deal with. Events starts slowly at preparation and as the event date nears, the workload builds up until the day when planners are busy running about to make sure everything goes well. If you don't manage this effectively with your team, then you burn out. If pressure is not managed appropriately, you make bad decisions.

The event planner is a good manager who must of necessity be able to provide opportunity to develop, sharpen and test analytical skills in real world of management in the following areas:

- Assessing situations
- Sorting out and organizing key information
- Asking questions
- Defining opportunities and problems
- Identifying and evaluating alternative courses of action
- Interpreting data
- Evaluating the results of past strategies
- Interacting with other personnel
- Making decisions under conditions of uncertainty
- Critically evaluating the work of others
- Responding to criticism

To get a job done successfully on the event day, you will need to use a variety of management skills such as:

- Prioritizing
- Delegating tasks and responsibilities
- Coordinating
- Crisis management
- Recruiting and selecting people who can assist with the event
- Providing mentoring and support to employees and team members

Management procedures also include active participation, interaction, critical evaluation and effective communication.

Lack of managerial skill is the reason for failure to realize objectives. The more you practice the more proficient you become. Have a bold approach to management. The bottom line is the benefit outweigh the time taken to acquire relevant skills. There is need to know how to effectively manage finance as well as personal time.

Managerial abilities will enlist you as proficient, bearing in mind that your job is to provide a vision for your clients and make the vision come alive. Many are technically proficient but interpersonally incompetent. They might be unable to understand other peoples need or are poor team leaders.

The event planning process

Planning and managing successful event are a time consuming and complicated process. It can take many years of training and on the job experience for an event manager to become extremely effective at what they do.

One of the issues event managers faces is the vast number of activities and processes that are involved in planning and running events. Having the ability to multi-task is a must have trait. Figure 7.2 shows the various activities that may run through an event.

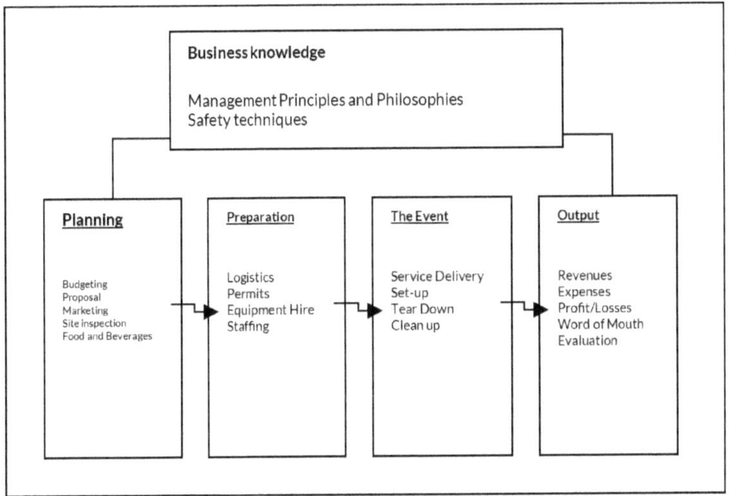

Figure 7.2 Event planning process

Event planning process combines organizational and interpersonal skills, as well as financial management and societal trends.

The aim is to set goals, develop strategies, outline task necessary for the event and ensure execution. This makes it is tedious hard-work that can run for days and being able to design, coordinate and execute the proposed event plans.

Running through an event requires adequate knowledge, planning and preparation time. You need ability to visualize concepts, plan the event, make profit and evaluate appropriately.

Before you begin choosing a venue, you need to know the basic parameters of the event. It is almost impossible to talk details and costs with a third party until you have the specifics ironed out.

Here are the key and details you should define before contacting outside vendors.

Date: Everything revolves around the date of the special event. Ideally you want to have three potential dates in mind so that you can compare availability and prices across the board. Try to include different days of the week for maximum flexibility.

Time frame: Event a single hour difference can make an impact on your planning, so you really need to get specific about the anticipated time frames. For examples starting at 10am instead of 8am means you may not need to allocate a breakfast budget.

Budget versus costs: It might sound impractical to work on a budget before knowing venue and catering costs, but working this way provides a benchmark for you to measure all of vendor proposals.

Begin with your revenue sources. How much should you charge for attendance? Will you call on sponsors to help offset costs? What will exhibitors pay to participate? Revenues will ultimately dictate your budget, so it makes sense to project them first.

Marketing: After you have identified your revenue sources, the next step is to outline your marketing plan. What is the best way to reach and engage your revenues and generators? This will be discussed in a later chapter.

The benefits of this process are as follows:

a.   Time saving

It's important that the Event manager has a clear and efficient process they adhere to when running events. Creating processes that others can follow also means that other team members can assist or take over the management of an event with ease. Many Event planners will create and update their processes with each event more effective and efficient. Having a set procedure that is put down means the event can be managed far easier.

Being efficient in the Event planning process also helps with event analysis.

Personal time management skills are essential for professional success in your workplace. Those able to successfully implement time management strategies can control their workload. In such a situation the stress involved in long hours of multi-tasking declines and personal productivity soars.

b. Saving

The common phrase "time is money" is extremely applicable in event management. Having an event manager who is effective at their job, and who understands and follows best practice event management processes and who has good relationships with efficient suppliers is a vital part of generating a high and fast ROI.

c. Improved event performance

Being able to efficiently run events also has an impact on the performance of the event. Delegates will have an improved experience if the event runs smoothly and without errors.

Event efficiency issues are likely to be poorly managed with errors and mistakes causing delegates to have unsatisfactory experiences. Ensuring that you provide the best possible experience for delegates is vital for the success of future event.

A key part of successful events is building up reputation in the industry and generating a long list of loyal, repeat purchase delegates.

When working on corporate event, planners help their clients to organize programs that focus on the purpose and message they are trying to communicate, the more "outstanding" your services are, the easier it is to convince clients to give their events to you as the expert.

There are also different stages involved in planning an event and all events should at least have this quadrant shown below.

An example of a typical event planning process is as shown below in figure 7.3.

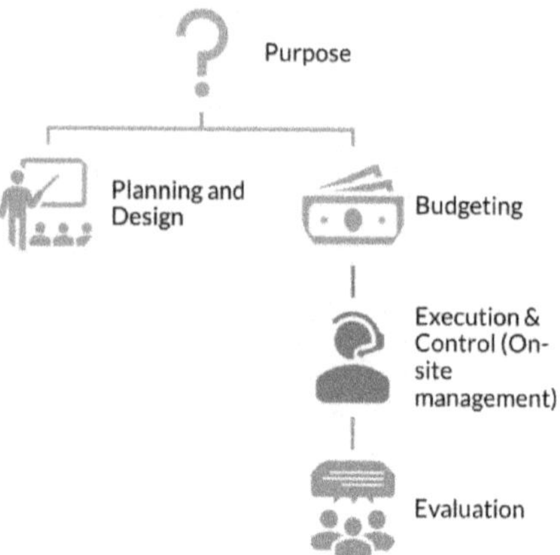

Figure 7.3 Event stages

When planning an event, it is important to follow through the aforementioned process in the sketch but we should know that each event is different from other in terms of the type of event, purpose, scope and size, to the budget of the event. Proactive planning by event organizers means nothing should be left to chance. Good planning means being prepared well in advance and ensuring that safety is a priority throughout the event.

In employing our workforce, we should be able to achieve a fit between persons and their jobs that fosters both high work and a high productivity and a high –quality organizational experience for the people who do the work. Two techniques for moving in this direction are job enlargement and job enrichment.

Job enlargement is the process of combining two or more specialized tasks in a work flow sequence into a single job. When using the technique of job enlargement pay and performance should be kept in balance to avoid boredom and alienation.

Job enrichment is redesigning a job to increase its motivating potential. Job enrichment increases the challenge of one's work by reversing the trend toward greater specialization. This introduces planning and decision-making responsibility normally carried out at higher levels.

Jobs can be enriched by upgrading five core dimensions of work:

1. Skill variety: The degree to which a job requires a variety of different activities in carrying out the work, involving the use of a number of different skills and talents of the person
2. Task identity: The degree to which a job requires completion of a "whole" and identifiable piece of work; that is, doing a job from beginning to end with a visible outcome
3. Task significance: The degree to which the job has a substantial impact on the lives of other people, whether those people are in the immediate organization or in the world at large
4. Autonomy: The degree to which the job provides substantial freedom, independence, and discretion to the individual in scheduling the work and in determining the procedures to be used in carrying it out.
5. Job feedback: The degree to which carrying out the work activities required by the job provides the individual with direct and clear information about the effectiveness of his or her performance.

Each of these core dimensions deserves a closer look. See figure 7.4.

How job enrichment works

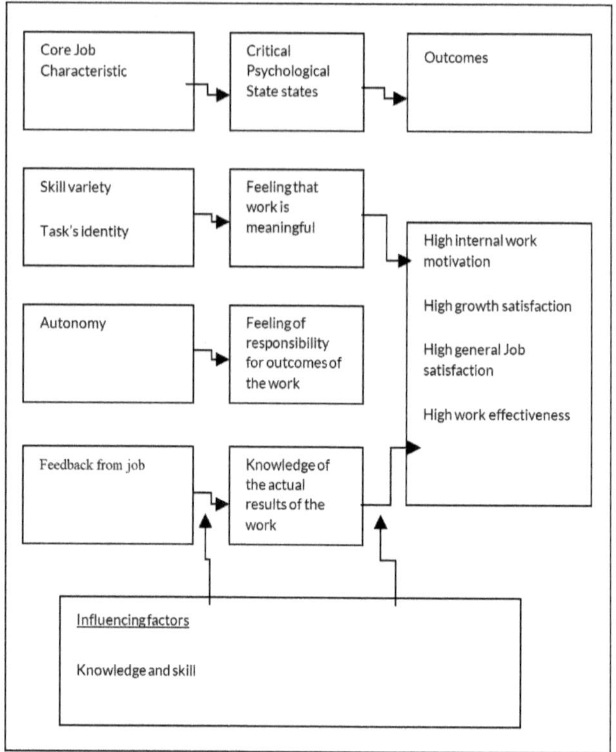

Figure 7.4 Work design log

Source: Management Sixth Edition (1995)

Effective team

Working effectively as part of a dream team is incredibly important for output quality, morale and retention.

Every event project must have an effective team. Any event takes a concerted team effort to handle all of the detail. Team doesn't just happen – they must be built. In a team, members may be involved in but not committed to the activities to the majority. Consider identifying one key event manager as well as individual persons for subcommittees such as venue manager, speakers, entertainment, publicity, sponsors and volunteer management.

Every activity carried out in this profession is done in teams. It therefore becomes mandatory to have formidable teams. Teamwork means working together for a common goal. All planning and management require some estimating-how long a task will take, given the availability of certain resources. A primary role for planning is that those individuals who must implement the plan should participate in preparing it. Working together as a team helps to share common course. To work together there has to be support, openness, and interdependence, which will lead to mutual understanding and greater commitment. The work of the caterer an aspect of most events rendering for example is determined by the work of the serving staff. A series of operations is necessary to complete any task and those responsible for performing such tasks must work as a team.

The following steps should be considered when organizing an event project team:

- Decide what must be done, using work breakdown structures, problem definitions and other planning tools
- Determine staffing requirements to accomplish the tasks identified in the first step
- Recruit members for the project team
- Complete your project plan with the participation of team members
- Every team must deal with: goals, roles, responsibilities, procedures and relationship.

Be proud of your team and instil purpose into team members, speak with encouragement and reinforcing words and back- up with believable action.

Are you a motivator? You must be able to motivate people to work together towards the achievement of collective goals and objectives. This brings improvement of cohesion among and between all people in your workforce. Every work team generates positive synergy through coordinated effort. This positive synergy allows for increased productivity. You become successful by helping others to become successful. Your skills in effectively managing your team will create a better working environment and thus result in great events. True team leaders know who they are and the authority under which they function. They are team players who can trust team members, if you don't trust those you're working with; you don't expect anything from them.

There are ten (10) Cs of effective team work; these are commitment, competence, character, control, communication, creativity, consequences, coordination, context and clear expectation.

Characteristics of effective team

- People
- Roles
- Processes
- Goods

According to Michael Hammer, a management consultant in using football analogy to point out the value of a relatively flat organization says "each of the defensive and offensive players has a particular job, but it is executed by co-operating with team mates. A coach oversees the process of carrying out the team's game plan, assisted by offensive and defensive coaches. To respond to changing circumstances, each player must be responsive to several coaches. Sometimes personal initiative is required." Working alone reduces learning whereas working on team increases accountability. Peer pressure is a powerful force.

The event planner should be able to assist members in meeting event production goals, providing direction and support towards achieving quality goals.

Similarly, the event planner coaches team members to do their jobs perfectly and become a winning team. There must be synergy in executing event projects whether by new team or old team. This can be done through proper guidance and encouragement from the team leader and that is no one else but you. Winning teams are hardworking, dedicated professionals and they are consistently goal oriented. They always research events, plan, network, as well as execute and evaluate an event.

The result of teamwork is effective service. People that work hard and tend to do everything legitimately are best.

You will not lose your cool when you know what you want, why you want it and how to communicate what you want to your team. This is because it is your absolute responsibility to bridge the difference and move the team towards common understanding and acceptance of event goals, objectives and their individual roles. Show enthusiasm and diligence. Your team will thrive on the care and appreciation you show them by words and actions. Event planners should combat negativity and promote teamwork.

Team glory

- Team is about trust
- Team is about working together
- Team is about supporting each other to meet targets.

The bottom line is that everyone takes the glory for a good work done.

Your duty as the team leader is to provide instruction, guidance, advice and encouragement that will help staff and service providers and lead the organization towards its objectives.

Thinking out of the box, pulling all activities and Togetherness of purpose is how winning works. The only way winning works.

Tools and worksheets

These are basic tools necessary to help you plan your events. Tools make it easier to do things with more rest. Tools help in accomplishing assignment.

Examples of these are Timeline, schedule, checklist, catering worksheet, rental worksheet, volunteer worksheet. It enables you to collate the necessary service providers' information checklist.

Event schedule/ time-line

A timeline has dates on attached to each activity. It helps to know what will happen when.

Event planners should be able to guide clients through the planning process and keep them abreast of everything involved in the event.

Event schedule includes tasks, staff assignments and program notes or cues centring on the days preceding and the day of event. It is organized by time of day. It is an important aspect of event planning that is usually carried out at the beginning of the project event stage. Event planning must take into account what impact particular date of the event could have in the success of the event. Event schedule on the other hand includes tasks, staff assignments and program notes based on the day preceding the event. Build the event schedule by listing, in order, all the tasks that it is needed to be completed.

You do this by making a checklist of all the jobs that must be done the coming week. You should list them in order of importance and by such order execute the job. "As each day's job comes up and is completed, cross it out and lift another weight from your shoulders". When you make an activity to do list does not matter, what matters is getting into the habit of thinking out a schedule.

Assign duration to each task and allocate the required resources. It ensures that every aspect of the event is professionally implemented without oversight. An event planning time-line on the other hand will keep everyone on track and ensure important deadlines are not missed out.

Critical path

In event project multiple activities often feed into other activities this have made it a must for event planners to get acquainted with the critical path method scheduling. This was developed in 1957, to address challenges on complex project. It is one of the most used scheduling techniques which Event planners must adopt.

It is useful in planning, scheduling and managing project activities. It includes all work specified in the contract document including all expected activities of suppliers, and vendors. It provides Event planners with a graphical view of the project; the time required to establish an activity and also help to determine activities that will become critical to the project if not completed by the specified time. A critical path method is a network of events each one directly connected to other activities.

Steps to completing a critical path schedule

- Identify the activities needed to complete the project
- Determine the sequence of the activities
- Connect a network of the activities with logical coordination and planning requirement
- Slot in the completion time for each activity listed on step 1. It is one of the most important steps when preparing critical path method.
- Identify the longest possible path to complete all activities
- Update all progress

Critical path method helps you to plan all tasks that must be completed as part of an event project. They act as basis both for preparation of a schedule and of resource planning. During management of a project, they allow you to monitor achievement of project goals. They help you to see where remedial action needs to be taken to get a project back on course. It also helps to identify the minimum length of time needed to complete a project. It helps to determine deadline.

Critical path method is the process to plan and control projects where activity is known. This method is followed when the time of completion of activity is known. In critical path method cost of the project is taken into account and the lost.

Defining the critical path of pulling off a music festival includes securing agreement for band performances. A music festival is a festival featuring multiple musicians. The festival may also showcase second stage acts and have vendors selling goods and services to attendees. Planning and orchestrating the festival will take months of scheduling, meetings, designing and negotiations.

Identifying the critical path to the music fest-the activity that takes the longest to complete require making a list of tasks that must be accomplished and the time it will take to get them done.

This could include:

- Securing a venue, and making talent performance agreements and vendor agreements. The festival must also be advertised in time for festival goers to buy tickets and make transportation arrangement.
- Assign a letter to each task. Establish the length of time required to complete each task. Estimate a start and end time for each task. Determine whether the completion of the task is dependent on another task. If so, write the letter associated with the prerequisite task.
- Create a chart that places the letter of each activity in a circle that is connected by a line to the next activity. The circles should be organized in sequential order. Add tasks that must be completed as part of another task in smaller circles that extend off the main circle. These activities are performed parallel to one another.
- Isolate the task that takes longest time to complete. Highlight the path to completing the path. The route to completion of this task is the critical path. Most often the critical path includes all the tasks necessary to arrive at completion of this one major task.

Gannt chart

The Gannt chart is a technique commonly used for planning work flow in event management.

The major features of the Gannt chart are:

- A listing of the tasks that must be completed

- The time frame for each task (the date on which the task must start and the date when the task must finish.

The Gannt chart has two principal benefits:

- The chart conveys complex information more easily at a glance
- The chart requires the event manager to go through the process of identifying tasks and considering timelines for each task.

Event timeline

A timeline is organized chronologically by date and may include tasks, staff, assignments, program notes and their corresponding deadlines. Time-lines are used as guides. The time-line will enable you stay informed as each part of the planning phase unfolds. Events starts slowly at preparation and as the event date nears the workload builds up until the day when planners are busy running about to make sure everything goes well. If you don't manage this effectively by using a timeline, then you burn out.

It is not abnormal to do list; this way you never have to bother yourself about your event success. It's a schedule of key tasks and dates clearly defined without fear of anything slipping through the cracks and you can be sure that this is easily usable. The event planner guides the client through the event planning process and keeps the client informed of everything involved in the event. With the aid of an event planning timeline, you can stay informed as each part of planning phase unfolds. This way you can never have to worry about your event success. When time is spent creating a detailed event planning timeline the event company team and the client can work together harmoniously without fear of something important slipping through the cracks.

You can successfully do this by [a] building a template [b] slotting in the necessary items [c] entering deadlines.

You must outline task to accomplish the event for month- to-month then week-to-week and day-to-day. It looks at the entire event planning process from start to finish.

Checklist

A checklist is a perfectly organized plan of action for any event. Having one will enable you overcome any obstacles to your objectives and increase the chances of meeting such objectives. Being able to prepare list is an excellent way to stay organized and accomplish goals. This tool is to make sure you have thought about the event and the planning involved. This is a list of everything you can imagine you have to do to achieve your goals. It is a generic checklist, so all questions may not apply. It gives a track on which to run on and is a good way to avoid missing any little details, which, when overlooked can negatively impact the program. It contains all the elements needed for effortless event production. A checklist will help you stay organized. Having it is an important way to increase productivity.

Your duty professionally is to be in charge of all details that go into the organizing of an entire event from its conception to completion and a checklist should include all you can do and those you will need to out-source to service providers. Ensure you have a checklist for every event; this will make for right choices especially choice of what they desire for their project to be effectively executed.

When planning events, the game rule is to under compromise and over deliver.

PRIOR TO EVENT

- Have you identified the purpose of the event?
- Have you secured funding sources?
- Have you identified your target audience?
- Have you reserved an adequate facility?
- What kind of set-up will you need?
- Are you expecting people with disabilities?
- Will food be served?
- Has food been ordered?

- Is security needed?
- Have you properly publicized your event?

Start two weeks ahead with advertisement, posters, and news releases?

- Are you sending out invitations?
- Do you need name tags and/or tickets?
- Have committees been formed and formed and duties assigned?

ON THE DAY OF THE EVENT

- Has the facility and set-up been checked?
- Have supplies been checked?
- Have you confirmed that workers will carry out their assignment?
- Have you thanked everyone involved?
- Have you collected invoices/receipt for financial tracking purpose?

AFTER THE EVENT

- Has a program evaluation been completed?
- Have "thank you" letters been sent when appropriate?
- Have all bills been paid?
- Have planners of the event gotten together to discuss how everything went, and made suggestions for improvement?

The following are steps that can be systematically adopted when organizing a community event and should include projected timelines for each step:

- Select members of your planning committee
- Plan the event
- Develop a master plan and set event date
- Have a workable budget
- Select subcommittees to be in charge of refreshments, setup and clean up, traffic and safety, invitations, volunteers etc.

- Formulate a publicity plan based on available budget. Decide when/how media should be contacted
- Prepare program copies and printed materials
- ·   Hold a "tie down" meeting the day before the event. Discuss assignments.   Answer any questions
- Distribute a program as guests arrive, so they know what to expect
- Remember to thank everyone who participated
- Conduct an evaluation
- Get the right people for the right activity, with the right communication and promotional activities in place.

A checklist will help you to create relevant activities aimed towards satisfied customers but it will not work out itself. Having in mind that the main reason you get hired is to organize events professionally. Being an effective organizer means paying attention to all the little details.

Chapter Eight

Marketing

Two major concerns for people starting a business are marketing and management. While marketing is an activity directed at satisfying the needs and wants of customers through exchange processes which occur in the market, management tend to focus on providing guidance and solutions in critical management issues to ensure business gets done efficiently through managing people and other resource. Marketing is preoccupied with the idea of satisfying the needs of the customer by means of the product and the whole cluster of things associated with creating, delivering and finally consuming it. In other words, marketing begins with the customer - these are the people who make your business successful. This is where the marketing process begins not with a new idea or innovative product. Entrepreneurs are always naturally enthusiastic about their ideas and assume other people will feel the same, but it doesn't always work that way. You will need to persuade many people that your service is worth buying, so it helps if you know a bit about them first. What are their problems, needs and wants? Can you help save their time and money or effort?

What matters for well – being is not just the characteristics of commodities consumed, but what use the consumer can and does make of the commodities.

In marketing you are exchanging offerings that have value for customers, clients, partners, and society at large. It means doing your homework, researching the consumer and writing a marketing plan.

In the world of the business, success stands above every other thing. Part of success is learning how to identify people, characteristics and loop holes. Your competitor is always the person that you are trying to close a deal with. They may become your pal once you have succeeded. Picture yourself as a chess game player with the. You have to calculate your risks, estimate your next move, and be watchful of your competitors move. Bearing in mind you have so many competitors competing for a slice of the market, you really need to put some effort into standing out of the crowd. As in the case of the chess game, if you miss one little thing you could lose your hold on the chess board and down goes the king.

Frequently used competitive approach:

1. Striving to be the industry's low-cost producer
2. Pursuing differentiation based on such advantages as quality, performance, service, styling, good value and
3. Focusing on a narrow market niche and winning competitive edge by doing a better job than rivals of serving the special needs and taste of the buyers.
4. Internally, business strategy involves taking actions to develop skills and capabilities needed to achieve competitive advantage.

Successful business strategies usually aim at building the company's competence in one or more core activities crucial to strategic success and then using the core competence as a basis for winning a competitive advantage over rivals.

A core competence is something a firm does especially well in comparison to rival companies. Core competence can relate to customer services, sales and distribution: or anything else that is a competitively important aspect of creating, producing or marketing the company's product or service.

A core competence is a basis for competitive advantage because it represents specialized expertise that rivals don't have and cannot readily match.

As with other industries, word of mouth is key and persuasion is a must. What is the customers' problem, needs and wants that requires your solution? Can you help save their time and money?

Marketing is a companywide orientation that put the customer first. Your business will grow faster when you are able to create new ways to market it. Marketing is a business culture that ensures focus on current and potential clients. It is a planning process. This means:

- Identifying opportunities and developing a strategy
- Using established marketing tools to deliver the strategy
- Measurement of your results and a process of continual improvement
- Understanding potential customers and the external business environment in as much detail as possible.

What is crucial to event companies is to ensure that the customer is at the very core of your vision throughout all departments and understood by every one of your employees.

Marketing concept

The marketing concept holds the key to achieving its organizational goals consists of the company being more effective than competitors in creating, delivering and communicating customer value to its chosen target markets.

The marketing concept has been expressed in many colourful ways:

- Meeting needs profitably
- Find wants and fill them
- Love the customers, not the product or service

The marketing concept rests on four pillars: target market, customer needs, integrated marketing and profitability.

Target market

Companies do best when they choose their target market carefully and prepare tailored marketing program. Carve out a niche and work it out.   Perhaps you have a list of potential attendees for an event say a workshop. That would probably be helpful, but what about sponsors or exhibitors? Targeted marketing campaign cost money, and that cuts into your revenues.   It is costly and time consuming to try to market your services to everyone. Focus your marketing effort on your target market.

Marketing plan

In today's competitive market place, you will need a marketing plan for your business.

Marketing plan is the representation of the ideas which the organization will put in place to ensure it accomplishes its objectives and attain its goals within a period of time.

To help market your event planning business effectively you need to find out how much business is necessary to cover all your cost and how much time you should be spending on marketing. But make certain when you start to do a lot of marketing in the format that your business can cope with the increase.

Game plan

What segment (clients or events) will be your market?

- Are there any segments you won't pursue?
- What are your personality strengths?
- What are your business skills?
- What is your education/training as it relates to event planning industry?
- What are your areas of expertise you will do yourself, what will you broker?
- What are your experiences and what did you learn?
- Who are established contacts, including vendors?

Part of any good marketing plan is laying out your business objectives. By writing it down, you are effectively dedicating your company to meeting that goal.

As you start your business brainstorm on ideas relevant for success. Imagine your business in five years. Ask yourself questions:

- What will my business look like?
- What will my revenues and profits be?
- How many employees will I have?

- What will my offerings look like?
- How many locations will my business operate in?
- How involved will I be as the owner?
- Will I include promotional campaigns?

Successful businesses invariably start with a marketing plan. Your plan should give clear-cut step by step actions to achieve your goals. If you don't come close to your goal by the end of the period, reassess your plan and make changes that are more realistic.

Just as your business changes your marketing plan should change too.

The plan should cover one year, the best way to think about marketing for small event companies. Things changes, people leave, market evolve, customers come and go. Later on, I suggest creating a section of your plan that addresses the medium-term future- two to four years down the road. But the bulk of your plan should focus on the coming year. It's not possible to do a marketing plan without getting people involved. No matter what is your size, get feedback from all parts of your company. This is essentially important because it will take all aspects of your company to make your marketing plan work. Your key people can provide realistic input on what's achievable and how your goals can be reached, and they can share any insights they have on any potential, as yet –unrealized marketing opportunities, adding another dimension to your plan. If you are a one- person management operation, you'll have to wear all your hats at one time- but at least the meetings will be short!

The event planner should understand the customers' taste and want. The clients I have been fortunate to work with have enabled me to know exactly what we should opt for before we start- up. You need know that events are good avenues to find clients, but you should find a niche for yourself. Set your standard high, but attainable.

Ingredients of a marketing plan

A business plan can be formal (if you a presenting it to investors or a bank) or informal (if it is just for your reference), but whatever style you write it in, there are certain component you should include.

- Executive Summary
- Business Concept
- Financial Details
- Financial Requirements
- Current Business Status
- Major Achievements

The benefits of a marketing plan

CHART TO SUCCESS: How can you possibly know what's going to happen 12 months or five years from now?   As I stated in an earlier chapter if you don't plan you are doomed, and an inaccurate plan is far better than no plan at all.

Rallying point: Your marketing plan gives your troops something to rally behind. If you want your employees to feel committed to your company, it's important to share with them your vision of where the company is headed in the years to come. People don't always understand financial projections, but they can get excited about a well –written and well- thought – out marketing plan.

Top level reflection: In our daily competitive business environment, it is hard to turn your attention to the big picture, especially those parts that aren't directly related to the daily operations. You need to take time periodically to really think about your business- whether it's providing you and your employees with what you want, whether there aren't some innovative wrinkles you can add, whether you're getting all you can out of your products and services, your staff and your markets. Writing your marketing plan is the best time to do this high-level thinking.

Captured thinking: Financial reports are the lifeblood of the numbers of the side of any business, no matter what size. It should be no different with marketing. Your written document lays out your plan. If people leave, if memories falter, the information in the written marketing plan stays intact to remind you of what you have documented.

In your marketing plans identify the following and whatever you need to implement into your plans critically.

- Who are you trying to attract by this I mean who are your customer base?
- Do you need posters, banners or flyers? And if needed, what number do you intend printing?
- Do you need to send a press release to launch into the industry?

Once you have established a solid marketing plan work an event or two into your promotional schedule which implies that planning an event can be an excellent way to promote your business.

The best way is to provide prospects with programs that will attract not just any customer but the right kind of customer. Your business will never grow beyond its capacity to meet needs.

Company operational instruction

Your marketing plan is a step-by-step guide for your company's success. It's more important than a vision statement. To put together a genuine marketing plan, you have to assess your company from top to bottom and make sure all the pieces are working together in the best way. What do you want to do with your company in the coming year? Consider it a to-do-list on a grand scale. It assigns specific tasks for the year.

Ideally, after writing marketing plans for a few years, you can sit back and review a series of them, year after year, and check progress of your company. The marketing stage is where you will meet the people who will help you succeed– the customers. It is good to research your targeted audience and uncover a few potential customers; but you will need more than that to succeed.

If marketing is seen as the task of creating, promoting and delivering great services to clients then this has to be creatively done. There is always a market for different experience. The event planner needs to become a brand and should be able to analyse market opportunities which will help her identify core competencies, market experiences and give to customers "the best solution".

There should be a balance between marketing and promotional activities. Decide on the style of marketing that best match your target audience. Determination and diligence are the key word to adopt when in search of success. Greatness won't just happen by fluke; it has to be consciously attained. Professional event planners know about relevant marketing information that culminates into success such as making sure their social programs are packed full and they integrate with as many social networks as possible. They also make sure those who attend their events relax and enjoy some nice time. Spending much money on marketing is a waste if you can't give your customers what they want and more importantly what they expect.

Appraise yourself to know if you have the drive and skills to market your business in the right direction. Be ready to move and market your business when you are starting new. Plan on marketing yourself for several months before you get a client or customer base of sufficient size and stability. Use social media channel that is conducive to your audience as could also create lack of interest when they are not comfortable with the media. Ask questions like how can we improve the event? Or what do you like about the event to get better feedback. Maximize interest and minimize questions.

Every marketing process involves (a) planning marketing programs (b) organizing, implementing and controlling the marketing effort (c) developing marketing strategies and (d) analysing market opportunity. Clients patronize event planners mainly for satisfaction of needs and exclusiveness. If you break a promise to a client for example you lose customer loyalty.

Event marketing

This is the activity of designing or developing a themed activity, occasion, display or exhibit (such as sporting event, music, festival, fair or concert) to promote a product, cause or organization. Events are a good opportunity to find contacts and clients.

Marketing ideas are important for success and having marketing skills is necessary for pricing, promotion, and event delivery. Marketing is often seen as the driving force for organizations.

In the world of business, success stands above every other thing. Part of success is learning how to identify people, characteristics and loop holes. Your opponent, is always the person that you are trying to close deal with.

Event marketing is using the media for promoting, marketing or advertising your event. It is a popular and productive way to build your business. It is not like doing book work but a practical knowledge of how you propose to reach your customers. Marketing is influenced by internal and external environment.

The marketing environment has three key perspectives (a) Micro-environment that influences the organization directly (b) Macro-environment that can influence the organization indirectly (c) Internal environment that is internal to the organization.

To foster teamwork among all sessions, the company carries out internal marketing as well as external marketing. External marketing is marketing directed at people outside the company. Internal marketing is the task of hiring, training and motivating able employees who want to serve customers well. Internal marketing must precede external. It makes no sense to promise excellent service before the company's staff is ready to provide it.

Corporate event marketing can be seen as the act of designing a theme activity, or exhibit such as music festivals, fairs and consumer carnival, to promote an organization. Events like seminars, conventions and fund-raisers could also be used to engage prospective customers, build awareness or market a company's products and services. One good example of Event marketing is trade show marketing whereby your business purchases booth space and present your company's product or services to trade show attendees. Event marketing avails any company the opportunity of moving from one- on-one basis of selling to group selling. Group selling lets your company presents its products to several prospects at the same location or at the same time.

Relationship marketing

Building strong relationship for business growth is one major task for event planners because it is a great way to brand building.

The trust bridge to relationship building often takes more than one shot to develop. One of the relevant skills for building critical business relationships is the ability to think strategically about who is worth knowing about our services. Strategic relationship building means identifying a small set of people who are in powerful positions and whose help could advance your business interests. Some influential people could be unresponsive to your advances; but constant approach can build up confidence.

You should target an audience that suits the information on services and strive to retain customer's interest. Relationship marketing can be applied when there are alternatives to choose from; when the customer makes the selection decision; and when there is an ongoing and periodic desire for your services. This is vital not only with the clients but vendors and staff as well.

Relationship marketing and customer service are inseparable and it is a purer form of marketing. A key principle of relationship market is the retention of customers through varying means and practices to ensure repeated patronage from preexisting customers which is important to the event planner.

It has been discovered that:

- Long – term customers tend to be less inclined to switch, and also tend to be less sensitive with price.
- Long – term customers may initiate free word of mouth promotions and referrals.
- Customers that stay with you tend to be satisfied with relationship and are less likely to switch to competitors,

making it difficult for customers to enter the market or gain market share.

You shouldn't have any problem asking questions designed to help you learn more about your customers. It is not a matter of throwing parties or entertaining people but establishing good rapport.

It is also vital to stay in touch regularly, to seize every opportunity, even for few minutes to ask what people are working on now and how their pet projects are going.

Strong relationship is your ability to work with clients and others, understand and motivate them both individually and in groups. Many are technically proficient but interpersonally incompetent. They might be unable to understand other peoples need or are poor listeners. Good human skills will help us to communicate, delegate and motivate others around us.

As you learn more about clients you will be clever to offer some gentle suggestions along the line.

Regular clients tend to be less expensive to service because they are familiar with the process, and require less education.

It usually involves providing more personalized service and providing quality service that exceeds expectations at each step. You can only attract people when there is a spirit to be accepted that means you don't fail to make others see their importance, worth and value.

Present your business to everyone you meet. If we truly value what we do and what we offer, it is only natural that we want to share these things to those we come in contact with because they are all potential customers. Conversation is your key to establishing the relationships that can translate into new customers. Make that initial connection and grow it into a lasting and sustainable relationship.

Coordination of effort is vital to a well- rounded relationship marketing strategy. To further enhance your marketing ability and to achieve objectives, note the following:

- Identify market opportunities and needs
- Keep abreast with relevant technological development as it relates to the business.
- Manage services professionally
- Advertise and promote your services when necessary
- Sell your services using word of mouth
- Set prices and terms of contract
- Plan the marketing activities and re-evaluate your marketing plans regularly especially the pricing and promotion strategy. Markets are always changing and you should adapt to both external and internal change.

Benefit of networking

There are many benefits to networking.

- It grows your business and help you gain better position in the market
- Networking allows you to be open in which case you gain more information for yourself and share information with others
- When you network you are being active connecting to people who can move you forward
- Networking helps you expand your knowledge and put you in a position to help others
- When you network you gain new leads
- At networking events you are sure to make great new business contacts and connections.
- Networking is a marketing skill in itself, the more you network the better you do and the more chances there are that you will grow.
- Networking helps to improve your reputation and a good reputation leads to support.

Results may not happen overnight; it takes time to develop a two- way dialogue and truly understand the needs of others. Networking is not an instant gratification.

Branding

The American Marketing Association define a brand as a name, term, sign, symbol or design or a combination of them, intended to identify the goods or services of one seller or group of sellers and to differentiate them from those of competitors.

Branding is a means of communicating what to expect from your event planning company. A brand is an offering from a known source. Brand awareness requires fore-thought and attention to details.

The most distinctive skill of professional event planners is their ability to create, maintain, protect and enhance brands. In essence, a brand identifies the seller or maker. It sets one company apart from another. It tells us what we can expect from that company. It's about the perception people have of the company. Brands build name, awareness, prompt customer selection and help a business in attracting and retaining highly skilled employees and also differentiate products and services from competitors. As someone said, brands plants love marks in the minds and wallets of customers which make selling easier as a result of this connection and this contribute to profitability.

A brand is what sticks in your mind associated with a product, service or organization. It can be a name, trademark, logo, packaging, colours and reputation for customer service, speed, self - serve options, low price, and high quality, whatever. Does a picture pop into your mind about a company, such as its logo or colours? Sometimes is not the logo but even packaging. For small event companies what sets apart the business may be factors such as high quality, craftsmanship, personalized customer service, superior knowledge to help customers make the proper product selections and similar factors.

A brand is essentially a seller's promise to deliver a specific set of features, benefits, and services consistently to the buyers. Branding is something that triggers associations in our minds. It is about creating

an identity and it conveys a uniform quality, credibility and experience.
See figure 8.1.

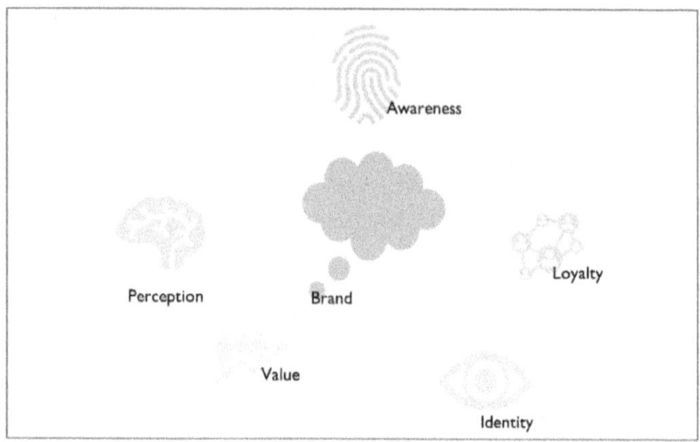

Figure 8.1: The Brand

Branding is what creates customer loyalty.

Your business name is a brand that should effectively deliver the
message and confirm to your target customers that you are credible,
that implies that the name should be memorable and easy to
pronounce. You must reflect the image of your establishment. For
me, this was the hardest thing I had to do when setting up my
business. I brain stormed several possibilities, until a nomenclature
that truly represented what I had to offer was deduced.

When you are deciding a company name, think about the images it
conjures and how you might use that to develop an identity or a
"signature" that is all yours. Your business name is your image and
your image is everything you need for uniqueness. My business name
came out of inspiration and is called "Movina Professional Managers."
We do more than what can typically be thought of as events. A good
name will add to your professional identity.

Every brand contact delivers an impression that can strengthen or weaken a clients' view of your company. Brand strength is in strong favourable brand name while the service you offer, experience, personality, and information available to you are offerings that satisfy a particular client need.

Image is that mental picture, generally called to mind when your firm's name is mentioned. Image can be enhanced through your activities and enhancing your image helps to erase negative impression which customers may have about your firm. There is also pricing issues. Pricing is easier to discover and compare than ever before.   When all prices are the same what makes the buyer choose one over another? Price, accessibility and availability of clean basic event supplies and high-quality service enhances image. Your company name should clearly deliver the message, connect your target prospects emotionally and confirm credibility. Brands are valuable. Building brands builds incredible value for companies and corporations. For small event planning companies, the challenge is how to get customers to think of them when it is time for event products and services. You don't want your company to be non-existent in your customers' mind. For such companies branding will assist and reinforce your sales and marketing efforts in important ways.

To help you create, build and reinforce brand you can try out the following:

1. Start with clarifying what your brand stands for. What is that "one thing" you want customers to think of when thinking of your company?

    Most knowledgeable- Your staff can help customers to choose options that best meet their theme

    Speed- Such as fastest time to create a customized solution

    High quality- Especially when all the competition is low quality.

If you and your team are confused about that "one thing" that sets your company apart, customers probably will be too. You can do a customer survey to ask existing customers what they value most. Then ask new customers what made them choose your company.

Try to limit it to one thing or at most two things you want your brand to be known for. Customers don't choose a vendor for twenty reasons. One or two things push them over the decision edge.

2. Demonstrate it with stories- Stories make your brand "stick." Show what you offer.
3. Audit your marketing materials- Check over your marketing piece. Do you have words in them to clearly convey "that one thing" that you want to be known for? Make sure everything reinforces what you want customers to think of your business.
4. Use colours, symbols and other elements to create visual associations. Check your marketing materials for consistency. Branding is not just for big corporations. When customers have seemingly endless choices, branding becomes a crucial competitive edge. That is the value for branding for small businesses.

It is worth knowing that in the face of the current economic challenges brands do better in tough times compared to unbranded company products. No branding, no differentiation, and no differentiation, no long-term profitability. People don't have relationship with products or services, they are loyal to brands.

Brands convey the following meaning:

a. Attributes: A brand brings to mind certain attributes, planners may suggest – exquisite, high-prestige event, luxury events and elaborate. Things no one actually needs, but so many desire.

b.   Benefits: Attributes must be translated into functional and emotional benefits
c.   Values: The brand may represent a certain culture such as Nigerian, Arabian, Philippine or Asian. Approach to customizing events.
d.   Personality: The brand can project a certain personality
e.   User: The brand suggests the kind of consumer who uses it

The most enduring meanings of a brand are its values, culture, and personality.

Event planners should know that branding is such a strong force that hardly anything goes unbranded today.

BRAND MANAGEMENT

Brand management is the process of maintaining, improving and upholding a brand so that the name is associated with positive results. Brand management involves a number of important aspects such as cost, customer satisfaction, in-store presentation, and competition. Brand management is built on marketing foundation, but focuses directly on the brand and how that brand can remain favourable to customers.

ADVANTAGES OF BRANDING

- Branding gives the planner the opportunity to attract a loyal and profitable set of customers. Brand loyalty gives planners some protection from competition
- Branding helps the planner to segment markets
- Strong brand helps the corporate image.

BRAND STRENGTH

The following are key brand strengths;

- Develop creative advertising
- Sponsor well-regarded events
- Provide well – appreciated public service
- Be known as a value leader

- Develop a strong symbol or spokesperson to represent the company

SEVEN CHARACTERISTICS OF SUCCESSFUL BRAND

The following are seven characteristics of a successful brand;

a. Audience knowledge
b. Uniqueness
c. Passion
d. Consistency
e. Competitiveness
f. Exposure
g. Leadership

Chapter Nine

Event safety and risk management

Event safety

Events have the ability to engender social cohesion, confidence and pride but event success is also measured in many ways by all of these factors and safety is one of them.

Since the terrorist attack in New York on September 11, 2001, threat of terrorism has resulted in increased security at major events worldwide. The success of any event is dependent on a safe, serene and welcoming environment for both attendees and organizers. This is an event held without theft, active shooting, stabbing, and electrical storm during an event, stampede, fighting and bomb blast and many other possibilities. In all cases of event planning a safety culture in management and operational practices is essential. From product launch to planning sporting events, come together seamlessly safety conscious event planners who play a critical role in the hospitality and entertainment industries. To this end they cannot be excused from the significant responsibility of providing the public with the highest standard of safety and security that is both possible and feasible at events.

They must first, foresee the nature of the crowd that will be in attendance. Second, they must be able to observe the behaviour of a crowd while an event is taking place and make timely decision for effective action. Finally, they must have the ability to establish policies, design and execute operations taking into consideration the configuration of the venue and the setup of the particular special event.

If event planners fail to consider disabled people when planning their events, they are ignoring a potential market base.

Event safety procedures

The event planners must ensure that event management procedures cover a full range of emergencies including major injury or illness of attendees, fire, bomb threat, crowd disturbances and climatic conditions such as lighting, torrential rain, flooding and much more.

Although the most important procedures will be about safety, there should be other procedures that lessen risks to the event profitability and the organization's reputation. The restriction of access to certain se procedures might include:

- Restriction of access to certain area in the case of a football event
- Arrival and greeting of visiting dignitaries
- Marshalling of competitors
- Raffle and fundraising
- Giveaway of merchandising or free food and drink
- Food serving and hygiene
- Waste collection at large events
- Cash management

The provision of training to event staff and volunteers is critical element in risk management and can't be overemphasized. It is a reasonable use of the event manager's time to have meetings with event staff, either individually or in groups to determine their knowledge of procedure.

Case study

The thrill of attending an event is usually followed immediately by concerns for safety. Will there be enough security? What if the crowd gets wild? Does the facility have proper means of evacuating should there be emergency?

These concerns are very valid and in fact were the highlight of the investigation following at City College. Security was lacking at an event that was to benefit AIDS charities featured hip hops moguls of the 90's. According to some reports the event was oversold. Another contributing factor to the stampede was the unusual layout of the National Holman Gymnasium. Gaining entrance to the Gym required going down a set of stairs and through four doors; three of which were locked. As the crowd surged forward, the earliest patrons to enter were caught in the doorway. Nine people died and twenty- nine or more were injured.

As a result of this catastrophe, Judge Louis C. Benza of the New York state court of claims issued a ruling placing 50 percent of the blame for those deaths on the venue's owner, the City University of New York, and 50 percent on the event's promoters.

After reviewing the circumstances that led to the tragedy, security experts expressed that the venue was poorly staffed. Ron Deisener, an experienced concert promoter said that for a younger urban crowd like the one at City College, he would have used one (1) guard to 50 fans. Other experts estimated that the number should have been closer to one (1) in thirty. The event utilized only one hundred and twenty-four (124) New York police officers; campus security and security officers combined to control more than three thousand (3000) attendees.

The event manager must take into account all elements of an event especially the type of event, characteristics of the facility, size, and demeanour of the crowd, methods of entrance, communications, crowd control and queuing having in mind that admittance into events range from free and open public admission to restricted admission.

It is extremely important for event organize to have an emergency plan in place.

The objective of such a plan would be to reduce the possible consequences of an emergency through the provision of training to event staff in:

- Awareness of types of emergencies at events
- Early recognition of an emergency situation
- Actions to be taken to bring in medical services (e.g. ambulance, medical personnel, first aid) to those in need
- Crowd communication, direction and control
- Accelerating the resumption of normal operations

An emergency plan specifies the organization's policies and procedures for handling sudden and unexpected situations which require immediate action.

Elements of an emergency plan

- An emergency plan should include the following elements with the appropriate documentation:

1. Assessment of the size and nature of the events foreseen and the probability of their occurrence. It is highly recommended that a vulnerability analysis be instigated.
2. Formulation of a plan in consultation with outside authorities such as emergency services, fire department, police.
3. Procedures
    a. Raising alarm
    b. Invoking the emergency plan
    c. Communication both within and outside the site
    d. Evacuation of non-essential personnel to pre-determined safe assembly points by pre-determined exits.
4. Appointment of key personnel and their duties and responsibilities
    a. Site incident controller
    b. Site main controller
5. Emergency control centre (if required)
6. Action on site, for example alerting staff and students, ordering evacuation, confirming evacuation is complete
7. Action off site, alerting external aid, advising the media
8. Where and how injured persons are to be treated. Are suitable first aid facilities on site?

- The plan should define the way in which personnel at the incident site can initiate action. The plan should also contain the full sequence of key personnel to be called.

- Emergency planning should consider the need to make arrangements for an authoritative release of information to the media. A person would be appointed to receive enquiries from the public.
- Appropriate training needs to be given to all personnel who are part of the emergency plan
- Once the emergency plan has been finalized and appropriate training has been conducted then the plan should be tested in one of three ways:
    a. Full scale exercise to test command, co-ordination and communication setups
    b. Tabletop exercises can be used to test some aspects of the emergency plan, and has the advantage of not interrupting normal operations
    c. Specific aspects of the plan can be tested, for example communication and evacuation.
- The emergency plan must be regularly updated. This will take into account changes in personnel, telephone numbers and storage areas. This requirement should be written into the plan, and should be the responsibility of a particular individual.

Risk management is an integral part of the event project as a whole and needs to be developed to go along with every other piece. Risk is a structured approach to controlling uncertainties and potential dangers at events by assessing what the particular uncertainties or dangers are, then developing strategies to mitigate those uncertainties. This is as a possible circumstance that can have negative influence on an event project. A risk can mean many things, but the main risk to consider are anything that could cause harm to another person, cause damage to equipment, infrastructure or the event site, or harm the effect of the organizers and event itself. Some risk may be out of the event organizer's control. In this case it is important that the risk management plan details the person responsible for coordinating the safety of every person should something that is out of control of the event organizer occur.

Importance of managing risk

Before you undertake any event project, it is crucial to identify project risk as it relates to the event, analyse and plan responses to manage those risks. The objective of this plan is to minimize the impact of threats, and increase the probabilities of opportunities. Risk to human safety: It is the planners' duty to implement strategy to ensure the safety and wellbeing of all event goers.

- Risk such as safe environment for participants, officials, volunteers and spectators at event sites.
- Sufficiency of resources such as equipment resources, manpower and facilities
- Injury Risk: Employees, persons who attend the event may be injured during the event
- Financial Risk: Events usually require a large amount of funding.

Risk management process

You will agree with me that there is no business without its associated risk, but the ability to manage risk is what makes the difference. A risk assessment should consider;

- Existing risks of the site
- Risks that the event creates
- External risks that the event organizer has little control over but may need to be managed at the event.

There are some questions event planners should ask themselves when assessing risks of an event.

- Will there be moving vehicles near the event site and could this pose a risk to pedestrians?
- Is there anything on the site that could become dangerous if there is inclement weather?
- Is there a body of water near the event site?
- Is there infrastructure being brought onto the event site? Who will ensure it is safely secured?

- Will there be carnival rides at your event and how will the safety of event guests be ensured when on or near rides.
- In the event that evacuation of the event site is required who is responsible for ensuring all people are calmly and safely moved?
- Are the likely guests at the event at higher risk of requiring emergency services? If so, have you advised local emergency services?

A complete risk management process before event

This can include:

THE INITIAL RISK ASSESSMENT

- The developed risk control plan
- An emergency management plan
- Traffic management plan – where applicable
- Waste management plan – where applicable
- Site safety induction checklists – for staff working on the event or site. It is important to remember that every event is different and have different resources available.

The responsibility at an event usually rests on the shoulder of the planner that has been hired to orchestrate the planning and bringing the entire event together. How does the event planner protect themselves from the risks of the business? Due intelligence on all aspects of an event will pay off in the long run.

Identifying and analysing risk helps to discover the factors that may work against the success of an event project and to state ways of preventing such negative occurrences and discovering counter measures that would avert such negative effects. Risk assessment can also be considered by answering the following:

- What could happen in the process of event production?
- How likely is it to happen?
- How bad is it if it happens?
- How can you reduce the probability and by how much?

- How can you reduce the impact and by how much?

Developing an effective risk management plan is an important part of any project.

A risk management plan identifies all the potential risks that may arise from staging an event and then lists the steps event planners will take to reduce or mitigate identified risk. The objective of this plan is to minimize the impact of threats, and increase the probabilities of opportunities. Event planning and management is full of uncertainties like power failure, medical emergency, brawl, equipment failure, stampede, fire, sponsorship withdrawal, crowd disturbances, torrential rain and more recently bomb threat and active shooting. Risk could also arise from uncertainties in market prices, weather risk for outdoor events especially, equipment breakdown, delay in event supply and conveyance, last minute turned down by artist. Clients get frenzy over an event starting late due to entertainment errors, improper hall arrangement, and unavailability of certain equipment to mention a few.

For major events what should be considered is anything that

- Could cause harm to another person
- Cause damage to equipment, infrastructure or the event site
- Harm the future of the event organizing committee and event itself. It rests on the planner to carry out risk management at each and every stage of event production. For example, when risk management is done in the security management section, then it deals with stampede, brawl, bombing, active shooting and the like.

It becomes a heavy task for the event planner to deal with all these contingencies without a well thought out risk management plan. To relieve a planner, risk can be transferred by contracting and this decreases both risk and control on the part of the planner but it will require proper legal procedures where necessary or a duly signed contract where terms and conditions apply.

Event Management company

Events are full of uncertainties and only event planners with the right skills can handle whatever deluge, crisis and pressures that may arise at each and every stage of event production. How will you deal with all these contingencies without a well thought out risk management plan? It is widely accepted in today's business world that one of the most significant risks a business can face is damage to its corporate reputation and this must be handled appropriately.

Risk management in the information management field is about loss of data due to theft or hard disk crash or loss of data due to fire outbreak. An information management system will need to provide a way to manage and document emergency management activities and contingency plan and implementation based on scenarios for all important systems processes and dependencies.

There is risk associated with human resources, finance, marketing, quality management, attendees, food and beverages management, technical management, infrastructure, logistic, procurement and team management. All of these causes harm to people, damage to equipment, infrastructure or the event site, or harm the future of the event organizing committee and event itself. How do you develop a contingency plan that will identify alternative courses of action if circumstances change with time when you are ignorant of crisis management skills? This step is most often procrastinated if everything goes on smoothly and without incident that approach does no harm. But normally, issues do arise and without well-developed plan, even small issues can become emergencies. Time of crisis is often defining moment for an organization. It is an opportunity to fail or succeed in managing events as they unfold. Sound event management and crisis management programs can significantly mitigate the potentially disastrous effect of any small- or large-scale event.

During a disaster you need a sound event management program that facilitates rapid communication, impact assessment and rumour control. Your investment in planning will help you manage even the largest long-term incident. Managing an event will require communication and decision – making system that will be able to quickly identify and respond to problems.

Of course, many risks are out of the Event planner's control. In this case it is important that the risk management plan details the staff responsible for coordinating the safety of every person should something that is out of control happen.

There are three processes involved in developing the plan:

- Identification of risks
- Analysis of identified risks
- Planning risk response

I will liken the role an insurance cover plays in the life of the insured to the role an event planner plays in the life of a client. When you pay for insurance, you protect yourself against something bad. When you hire an event planner the burden is taken off your shoulders.

Define your project

There is need to define your project. If you are responsible for the provision of information to a conference, the information gathering may not be easy. You can develop a risk management plan for the mitigation. This will be a simplified model where risk and impact are listed as high, medium and low.

Brainstorm on risk

It is advisable to get several people together that are familiar with the project and ask for input on what could happen, how to prevent it, and what to do if it does happen. The output of this brainstorming session will help in the following:

- Try to keep an open mind about ideas. "Out of the box" thinking is good but stay focused and on target.
- Identify the consequences of each risk. From the brainstorming session, you gather information about what

would happen if risk materialized. Associate each risk to the consequences arrived at during the brainstorming session.

- Eliminate irrelevant issues
- List all identified risk elements. List them one by one.

Assign probability

For each element on your list, determine if the likelihood of it actually materializing is high, medium or low. Note if the probability of an event occurring is zero, then it will be removed from consideration. There is no reason to consider things that simply cannot happen.

Assign impact

Assign impact as high, medium or low based on pre – established guidelines. If impact of an event is zero it should not be listed.

- Determine risk for the element
- Be flexible in analysis

There is always the potential for risk and this makes it necessary to manage it before it happens. Risk can be managed by transferring risk to reliable event service providers.

A complete risk management process before the event can include:

- The initial risk assessment
- The developed risk control plan
- An emergency management plan
- Traffic management plan - where applicable
- Waste management plan – where applicable
- Site safety induction checklists – for staff working on the event or site.

It is important to remember that every event is different. The most important part of creating a risk management plan is that you can reduce possible risks as much as possible and have thought about what you would need to do in the event of an emergency during an event.

The unexpected will happen anytime in the course of managing an event. You can handle this in three ways:

- Sufficiency of lead time to organize an event, finance and facilities
- Allow yourself a little extra time.

Challenge yourself to beat the deadline you have assigned to yourself.

- Get back-up (that is extra help or support that you can get if necessary).

Manage crisis before they happen. If you have three hundred people assembled in a banquet hall, you need to have to vet and ensure that the property has safety and security mechanisms that I assume are in place especially if you look at it on a global scale.

Before and during the event

Attendees should receive electronic or paper handouts about health requirements emergency preparedness and nearby medical facilities.

Conduct security audit on special event venues in the site selection process which include recording the number of placements of exits and assessing room capacity, the flow of people and available onsite emergency services. There is always the potential for risk. It is how you go about handling it.

Risk management is a very important aspect of event management therefore it should be carried out in a planned and professional manner.

Some common strategies used for risk management are:

- Risk Avoidance
- Risk Retention
- Risk Transfer
- Risk Reduction

Planners must take responsibility for their actions in business. Consequently, it is the planners' responsibility to advise their clients accordingly.

The responsibility of an event rest on the person or company hired to orchestrate the planning and bringing all areas together. Everyone from the stakeholder, the venue, the caterer, decorator and anyone else will go to the planner for answers when something goes awry. Every event is different and it is important to determine all of the risks possible. Learn as much as you can about the stakeholders, the event itself and anyone else who may be involved. Hire other companies to look after specific areas.

Consider having a sound and trust worthy law firm. There may never be a need to use a law firm for anything other than doing your corporate documents, but they are there to advise you in other matters as needed.

Event security

Crowd control and management

Managing crowd involves significant risk. The extent, severity and exposure to risk will vary depending on: the circumstances crowd controller finds themselves in; how well is crowd control staff been prepared; and how effectively risks have been controlled. The planner owes those attending the event "duty of care. "People attend an event for a specific purpose, effective crowd management adds to the fun of the event and can reduce risk of injury.

Crowd management must take into consideration all elements of an event especially the type of event, characteristics of the facility, size and demeanour of the crowd, method of entrance, communication, crowd control and queuing. As in all management, it must include planning, organizing, staffing, directing and evaluating. Particularly critical to crowd management is defining the roles of parties, involved in the event, the quality of the advance intelligence and the effectiveness of planning process. Choosing appropriate security is essential in the success of an event and the safety of the public.

Different types of events require different types and combinations of security.

Four conditions that can create crowd management problems:

- Problems created by a crowd from within
- Problems created for a crowd from outside
- Environmental catastrophe
- Rumour

These threats must be considered by those responsible for managing crowds. Most problems with crowds can be prevented or quickly resolved when all aspects of crowd management are well organized. Event planners should know that when large groups of people gather in any given place, they can cause havoc and create unsafe conditions for themselves and those around them.

The crowd control officers must receive comprehensive training on matters that deal with controlling the crowds such as:

- Security Barriers
- Directing traffic
- Power of words
- Body Language
- Identifying gang affiliate
- Recognizing aggression
- Dispersing of crowd
- Escorting of unruly individuals

Crowd safety is primarily a management responsibility and requires the application of the best practices of health and safety management. All who run venues, organize events or manage places which attract crowds should have a health and safety management system which anticipates monitors and controls potential crowding risks.

Provision must be made for patrons to queue and gain access to the venue and once the venue is to capacity, security officers should be available to control and monitor crowds at event entrances to ensure that crowd numbers are not exceeded, and when tickets are in use ticket revenues must be protected and waiting crowds remain well behaved.

Security officers must remain on duty until the conclusion of the event and orderly dispersion of the patrons.

Choosing appropriate security is essential to the success of an event and the safety of the public. Different types of events require different types and combinations of security. The event planner needs to examine the risks involved with the event by asking for example "what could happen" or "what if"? The answer will determine whether police, private uniformed or other security is required. Then ensure that at least some security officers are female for appropriate access to female toilets, dressing areas and for access.

Security officers should remain on duty until the conclusion of the event and orderly disperse of the patrons. Security should be extended to other nearby properties likely to be affected by the operation of the event. Security to protect the stage, mixing desk and lighting scaffolding should be considered by the event planner to ensure patrons do not climb on such structures, resulting in injury or damage to equipment.

Provision must be made for patrons to queue and gain access to the venue s to capacity, security should be available to control and monitor crowds at event entrances to ensure that crowd numbers are not exceeded, ticket revenues are protected and waiting crowds remain well behaved.

In the case that the event features an entertainment stage, it is essential to ensure that the event planner has barriers installed to ensure that patrons will not be crushed against the stage and barriers are placed in front of the loudspeakers so that patrons are at least one meter clear of the loud speaker. Security officers should also be present between the barriers and the stage to ensure no one compromises the security of entertainers.

Security plan

Developing a security plan with the security provider will clarify roles and responsibilities of security staff. The attitude of the security personnel must be friendly and professional in order to help maintain a positive atmosphere among patrons. The main responsibilities to consider are crowd control, cash protection, equipment protection, and procedure for confiscated or prohibited items.

To enable security personnel to perform their duties effectively it is vital that they be briefed appropriately prior to the event. This briefing must provide security personnel with:

- Details of the venue layout, including coordination centre, entrances, exits and first aid posts
- Any potential hazards
- Details of emergency and evacuation plans
- Clear direction on the management of unacceptable behaviour
- Instruction for the operation of any on-site machinery and utility supply in case of emergency.

Security personnel must:

Be able to communicate with other security providers

Be able to communicate with each other and first aid personnel and each company that provides crowd control functions at the event must be a part of the planning for the event.

- Security considerations
- Loss of children or people
- Lost and stolen property

Pre and post event briefings with all event personnel to instruct all staff who is allowed restricted or unrestricted access to the event and event areas.

Chapter Ten

Quality service

Quality is delivered whenever your services as event planner meet or exceed the customer's expectation. Your quality should include the knowledge of the business you have, promptness in service delivery, performance, reliability and efficiency. Whether the profit measure is return on sales or return on investment, event planning business with a superior service offering clearly outperform those with inferior service offering. Where superior quality and large market share are both present, profitability is virtually guaranteed.

In today's information hungry world, you can't afford to stop producing high quality content. If there is a gap, a lack, or a need, have enough spirit to admit where you are poor. Out of weakness comes strength if you work at it.

Total quality is the key to value creation and customer satisfaction. Value for money is especially important because in most markets there is room for service of different overall levels of quality and the client must be satisfied that the price fairly reflects the quality.

Finding new customers and keeping existing ones is very important. This can be done by offering quality service and bringing clients value in time and money saved.

Service enhancement is important to event planners. Good service means repeated business. In a competitive market, it is the customer who determines what constitutes a good or poor quality. Good quality helps to determine customer loyalty.

Best service quality encompasses the whole concept of an event planners' business. Every point of contact your clients have with your business will be measured in terms of quality of service.

From the telephone conversation, the face-to-face contact, to your mannerism, will all be assessed constantly in terms of the level of service your clients will demand and expect of you.

Quality service could also be in the area of creating impressive and successful event that have maximum impact. An event planner may win by delivering consistently higher quality service than competitors and exceeding customers' expectations. These expectations are formed by their past experiences, word of mouth and advertising. After receiving the service, customers compare perceived service with the expected service. If the perceived service falls below the expected service, customers lose interest in the planner. If the perceived service meets or exceeds their expectations, they are fit to use the planner again. Customers' expectations are the true standards for judging service quality.

Effectively managing expectations set the stage for surpassing them.

- We should strive to present a realistic picture of our service to customer.
- Performing the service right the first time should be a top priority in our companies. There is need for regular evaluation of our service designs
- Communicate effectively with customers
- Surprise customers during the service process

Once you have established a level of quality, it is important to improve and maintain it. Do not become complacent by allowing the standard you have set to become only adequate. Continuously monitor the quality of service; this will make your previous, current and potential clients to be able to help you achieve your objectives. Focus on delivering high quality service and win long term customer loyalty by {a} assessing situations, {b} sorting out and organizing key information, {c} asking the right questions, {d} identifying and evaluating alternative courses of actions, {e} evaluating results of past strategies, {f} developing and defending new strategies, {g} interacting with clients and other personnel, {h} making decisions under condition of uncertainty, {I} critically evaluating tasks.   Guarantee your clients of high-quality service that will give value for money saved.

Good service is having a compulsive need to win and hold affection of others. Prove your uniqueness all the way and your uniqueness are the problem you have a solution to. Life is a two-way street known as give and take. When you give quality services you earn recognition and fame.

Event planners face three tasks – increasing differentiation, service quality and productivity. Event planners often complain about the difficulty of differentiating their services. There is precipitated intense price competition. To the extent that customers view service provided as fairly homogenous, they care less about the provider than the price.

The alternative to price competition is to develop a differentiated offer, delivery or image.

Customer satisfaction

A customer is one who brings us wants, and it is your duty to handle them responsively and profitably.

Business fails when there is lack of sales. And of course, this refers to sales and resale. Customers and suppliers are to be empowered and motivated. If a business successfully creates and keeps customers in a cost-effective way, it will make a profit while continuing to survive and thrive. Your job as a business owner is to create and keep a customer. No matter what your official title is you are first a salesperson in your company. And the best way to increase your value as a salesperson is to build your customer base.

Think of the last investment you when purchasing something it could be a piece of jewellery. Think about the process that went into purchasing that item. Did you hunt around? What service did you encounter and was the service more important to you than the price? For most consumers, they will say yes. They'd rather pay more and receive exponential customer service than receive poor service and pay a cheaper price?

The best of both worlds is great service and best price, but if you can supply one or the other always side on that of providing the greatest customer service. You will never go wrong providing that service to satisfy customers.

A company makes money by satisfying customer needs better than its competitors. Consider the following case study:

The fast- food hamburger industry offers tasty but unhealthy food. The hamburgers have a high fat content and the restaurants promote fries and pies, two products in high starch and fat. The products are wrapped in convenient packaging, which leads to much waste. In satisfying consumer wants, these restaurants may be hurting consumer health and causing environmental problems. Situations like this one call for a new term that enlarges the marketing concept or call it the societal marketing concept which holds that the organization's task is to determine needs, wants, and interests of target markets and to deliver the desired satisfactions more effectively and efficiently than competitors in a way that pressure or enhances the consumer's and the society's wellbeing.

Customer satisfaction is believed to be a long-term strategy. The successful event planner cares first for the customers, then second for the services. It certainly takes time to create a reputation for service. Never reduce "customer satisfaction" for any reason.

There are quite a number of factors that can aid every event planner in attaining the desired success. These include:

- Courteousness of staff. Have you taken time to teach your staff the tenets of business?
- Method of handling complaints. You need an established policy that fits well. Handle complaints promptly and effectively.
- Quality service: If your company is quality conscious, it can charge some percentage higher than others.

- Customer loyalty results in high customer retention. Customer loyalty is the overall satisfaction that customers experience when doing business with you. It is the willingness to recommend you to others and the resistance to switch to a competitor.
- Efficiency in the area of bookings
- Table setting
- Making sure the purpose for the event is important enough to merit the time and expense needed to properly stage, publicize and evaluate the event.

This list however is in-exhaustive.

There should be no confusion as to what is your value proposition or value adding, it is simply what you offer and why the service is great for customers. This will garner tremendous profits for you. There are value turn offs that makes a customer never to come to you again.

Customer cantered event planner seeks to create high customer satisfaction rather than to suffer from high customer churn. Market success will accrue to only those that can deliver what the people want. The quality of services you provide will determine whether you get referrals and word-of-mouth advertisement. To ensure you are recommended, go the extra mile by advocating and practicing professionalism.

Event planners' offerings are transient but basic needs and customer groups endure for long. Never reduce "customer satisfaction" for any reason.

Parameters to judge success of an event

You can ascertain the success of an event by;

- Customer satisfaction
- Budget for the event
- Turnout for the event
- Numbers of potential business leads

To succeed in this business, you must understand:

- Industry trends
- People management
- Other analytical and creative aspect of the business.

Chapter Eleven

Ethical business practices

It is increasingly clear that having social and ethical problems is one of the greatest ways to erode brand value.

If there is any time to talk and teach Ethics that time is now. With the advent of social media many projects to the world what they are not making their reputation centre on what you can see on social media.

Ethics is a system of moral standard that govern you as a person. Every business has its ethics event planning inclusive. Transparency is a term that will be heard more frequently in business. Openness about business practices, policies, procedures and budget preparation with clients looking for full disclosures will be moving to the forefront in business world.

The ethical business owner is a confident business owner. It is easier to brag when there is nothing to hide. And honesty generates passion. As the owner of your business, you believe in the business and want to tell the world. So, when ethical behaviour generates both confidence and passion, you have a business owner who inspires trust. Trust with employees, suppliers, and clients.

"The truth shall make you free" is more than a platitude. It is an expression of how much easier it is to run your business when you use real numbers and honest budget for clients.

Clients will be looking to do business with event companies that demonstrate corporate responsibility, have no hidden agendas and whose business dealings are above board at all times. Good business practices and high ethical standards – both professional and personal will always work to build customer confidence and affect profits. Event businesses that demonstrate these qualities on a day – to – day basis and on all business, fronts will gain a competitive edge.

Although the business owner leads the enforcement process, all managers are expected to make a personal contribution by stressing ethical conduct with their subordinates and all team members and by involving the process of monitoring compliance with the code of ethics. "Gray area" must be identified and openly discussed with employees as well as team members, and procedures created for offering guidance when issues arise, for investigating possible violations and for resolving individual cases. It is never enough to assume activities are being conducted ethically, nor can it be assumed that employees understand they are expected to act with integrity.

You cannot have the "mentality to eat what you kill." This is because you know it is easier and more profitable to sell to an existing client than it is to sell to a prospect. Your company should always drive more repeat business. Bad behaviours lead to bad reviews, and that is bad business.

On the flip side when customers are treated ethically, word now gets around quickly. They come back for any event service thy desire and they make referrals. The business is not only rewarded with good ratings; it gets a boost to the bottom line.

There are established rules and codes of behaviour in this business which managers can exercise if there is one but where there is just a team lead, he can handle these procedures. First managers must set an excellent ethical example in their own behaviour and establish a tradition of integrity. Company decisions have to be seen as ethical. Second, managers and employees and all teams have to be educated about what is ethical and what is not: ethics training programs may have to be established and grey areas pointed out and discussed. Everyone must be encouraged to raise issues with ethical dimensions, and such discussions should be treated as legitimate topic. The event business owner should regularly reiterate its equivocal support of the company's ethical code and take a strong stand on ethical issues. Fourth, the event business owner must be prepared to remove people from a key position or terminate them when they are guilty of a violation. It also means reprimanding those who have been lax in monitoring and enforcing ethical compliance. Failure to act swiftly and decisively in punishing ethical misconduct is interpreted as a lack of real commitment.

Running this business is stressful but at the same time clients must know you love them and not just their pocket book. When you run your business ethically, you relieve stress.

Without a professional code, lines of acceptable behaviour are easily crossed bearing in mind that whatsoever you do personally can hurt you professionally. The client needs your knowledge, expertise, past experience but you need their money and friendship. Do not run-down other businesses to make a fast one. The fear of being caught pulling a fast one only adds to an owner's emotional turmoil. Adopting and owning a set of ethical standards not only is the right thing to do. It also reduces the owner's anxiety and improves personal health. We all feel better when we do what is right. Be a great event planner that treasure business ethics. Poor social and ethical performance in suppliers' chain impacts negatively on overall productivity.

Good reputation

Reputation is whom other people think you are and this picture may not really be you hence I'm using good reputation in my classification. This industry has got a history of lots of people entering it, doing a bad job, and then going bankrupt, so reputation is incredibly important.

A most vital asset in any business is its customers, without which we would not and could not exist. When we satisfy our, they help us grow not only by continuing to do business with you, but they also recommend us to friends and associates. It is necessary for us to identify the essentials required feat for success.

There is no successful business owner without character, integrity and commitment. When you lack character in business your expertise and brand is not genuine. You should put character above your business gains because it stabilizes your offerings. Many businesses are fast to maintain good image at the expense of character building. Character is really who we are, it has to do with cultural values, self -discipline, fortitude or good reputation. Your character will make you convincingly act on what you believe to be right all of the time. Character is what you do when nobody is watching. Our character very obviously influences our life, business, and our work and client's perception of who we are regardless of their character.

That is the reason Thomas Macaulay says "The measure of a man's real character is what he would do if he knew he never would be found out." Hence the supreme quality of a leader is unquestionably, integrity. Character is the beauty of life; it is your glory and your future. People will remember your character when you are gone. It should be treasured above styles and rewards. Your veracity must never be questioned since we are referring to an evaluation of your morals. Being able to implement the 3c concept of character, competence and consistency makes you great.

The basis of all good relationships and cornerstone of character is this one thing – can others trust you? Trustworthy people keep their promises and can always get the job done. Look for opportunities to go the extra mile and do more than you are paid for.

However, personal attribute and cultural values can never cover up for inadequacy of preparation and knowledge of business. But the truth remains that any event you plan and stage is a reflection of your character from the initial invitation to the on-site production. Run a number of successful events, build up good relationship in the industry and your reputation will soon tower over your competitors. For a start-up it may take two to five years as a rule to break even; five years doing good.

Make the right impression; you have only one opportunity to get it right. Don't seem to forget how important every single client and service provider is to your success in business. Being honest is a must have character in this business.

To build strong character you need integrity and self -discipline.

Having integrity is the job security you need, this talks about uprightness, sincerity and sound principles. Integrity means the quality

of being honest and morally upright. It is doing the right thing
because is the right thing to do. In business the only view that counts
are that of the receiver. People value sincerity. It is impossible to
build strong character without integrity. I mean integrity over personal
gains, integrity to people over things, to service over power, to
principle over convenience.

How to exercise integrity

Integrity is key to growth and a healthy enterprise. This is how to
exercise integrity:

- Meet your commitments
- Be honest to a fault: This means honest as seen by other
  people. Not telling the whole truth is dishonest.
- Treat everyone with respect: Make customers feel important
  and appreciated. No one likes to be dis-respected. All
  customers deserve common courtesy.
- Build and maintain trust: Trust is reliance relationship built
  on character, strength and ability. It usually takes several
  good acts to build, and one bad act to lose.
- Be consistent: Can your customers depend on you to provide
  a high level of service every time they choose to utilize your
  product or service.
- Offer better quality: Offer better quality than your
  competitors at the same price. Quality is whatever the
  customer says it is. Find out what your customers want and
  give it to them faster than your competitors.
- Know how to apologize: The customer may not always be
  right, but the customer must win. Deal with problems
  immediately and let customers know what you have done.
  Make it simple for customers to complain. As much as we
  dislike it, it gives us opportunity to improve.
- Give more than expected: How?
- What can you give customers that they cannot get elsewhere?
- What can you do to follow-up and thank people even when
  they don't buy?

- What can you give to customers that are totally unexpected?

Self - discipline on the other hand is doing what is right even when you don't feel like it. Doing what is right even when it hurts is important to event planners.

A good reputation is more valuable than money, says Publilius Syrus a Roman Philosopher. Without integrity true success is impossible.

Maintain sensitivity – speech pattern and personal mannerism, confidence in the services offered and communicating the services efficiently to clients. In situations where client is wrong in certain decision, you need to know how to give a benign smile, and advise decisively because you are the expert.

Cheating on clients is not smartness, is not only dirty but inhuman and degrading.

Always define clearly the client's expectations of what you will and will not provide by making bulleted list of specific services and products to avoid misunderstanding. Have regard to the terms of the contract or agreement.

Think through the great experience, the publicity, the relationship you will establish through each event by been ethical.

Always ask the question "what is the right thing to do in this situation."

Treat your clients like royalties. Never discuss their taste with other clients. This can be manipulated. I remembered discussing a particular client's taste for an event with another client and it was an expensive mistake that almost cost me that job. When character is absent, one of the richest jewels of life is forever lost.

Some suggestions to help maintain integrity:

a.   Practice good business ethics all the time and politely answer all enquiries from prospective clients

b.   Practice professional integrity by providing truthful and accurate information in all aspects of professional performance and duties

c.   Be responsible for your mistakes and learn from them

d.   Be a person who honours' your word

e.   Don't divulge information given in confidence

f.   Pay attention to details, double check for potential conflict of interest with clients and represent each client fairly and honestly

g.   Become known for doing what you say you are going to do and maintain the highest standard of excellence. Never try to be complacent with the status quo

h.   Deliver more than you promised and don't promise more than you can deliver

i.   Be honest; don't lie to cover facts. Walk your talk

j.   Update your clients periodically during a lengthy project and maintain a positive and professional attitude in all business relationships performing above the standards acceptable to this industry

k.   Be objective and tactful, promote and maintain the highest standard of personal conduct

l.   Keep receipts for specified vendors

m.   To buttress further, don't try to take on jobs for which you lack the necessary skills or expertise. Tell the client up-front if you believe the proposed task exceeds your capabilities.

n.   Keep professional relationships healthy and profitable. Don't tell lies to win any job. Many are doing greatly but crafty in all sense.

o.   Be consistently open and transparent all the way. It is going to take a lot of credibility for clients to hand you their pocket book for any event, and when they trust you enough to do so, be committed enough to do what they expect of you.

A great event planner assumes the role of an advisor, facilitator, mentor, budget manager and counsellor who gives clear instruction about what clients expect. It puts a demand on you to be a man or woman of integrity - broad-minded, intelligent, competent, trustworthy and charismatic.

Being ethical and sustainable is the business of today. Sustainability is about environment, social governance and ethics and all are crucial.

Win business in a highly competitive market using ethical business practices.

Unethical event planners will rationalize that they can handle all aspect of an event. Other ethical violations occur when event planners receive kick-backs from vendors as well as steal ideas from other event planners.

Some clients are also unethical they find faults and then demand a discount, but you need to be on guard. Some clients would engage more than one event planner or service provider in a bid to lower prices. A Japanese proverb says "The reputation of a thousand years may be determined by the conduct of one hour.

Principle of responsibility

The price of greatness is responsibility. True freedom demands responsibility. Responsibility is an internal feeling of ownership. It is the bed rock of leadership. Responsibility means "submitting or returning in submission, the power given to you." It is giving account of the ability to the one who sponsored you by maximizing the potential as he demands. A sense of responsibility is the clearest indication of maturity.

Taking responsibility has to do with making hard choices and doing the difficult things that will be required of you as an event planner. You are responsible for the entire project package this infers that the bulk of work depends on you, that implies that you are the one to be applauded or blamed. Be able to acknowledge and own up to errors and omissions. Admit your mistakes objectively since they are often correctable.   We all must rise up to the task of being responsible.

The opposite of accepting responsibility is making excuses, blaming others for what is not going right and becoming upset, angry and resentful towards people for what they have done or not done. Look for opportunity to go the extra mile and do more than you are paid for. When you do this enough you will eventually develop the partnership to the point where your competition doesn't have a chance against you.

Have respect for clients' right and beliefs. It is all about responsibility, intelligence and transparency on your part thus naturally clients begin to see you as a friend and an expert.

You are to focus only on your ideal outcome. Your responsibility is to ensure you do all that is expected of you. If otherwise, please take time to explain. Event planning is all about responsibility, intelligence and transparency. Responsiveness, pro-activeness, professionalism, value for cost and flexibility are a plus to your being responsible.   Get your act together and become responsible business owners. The responsible choice is always ours.

The more responsibility you accept, the more you cherish and value your assignment. Practice giving back to the society. Corporate responsibility is a must to every business owner. Champion a moral crusade that will establish in every stratum of the society the principles and virtues of loyalty, integrity, excellence and trustworthiness in business.

Take responsibility, don't blame others. Blame makes people not to learn and grow because you are not showing positivity to them.

Chapter Twelve

Personal management

What attributes makes you different from others? What makes your business unique? How best do you handle crisis? These are relevant questions for self- assessment. Personality impacts the management of people.

It is critical to understand that without the participation of other professionals in this field an event planner is incapable of performing all the relevant tasks. Planning and outlining goals for your life and business and then trying to fulfil these goals is very important.

Personal management helps to control time, manage finance and manage trend.

Event planners should make their appearance an asset. Your appearance communicates volume to people. Each professional event planner develops his/her individual style of running this business. It is necessary to attach your name and reputation to quality and image, as this will invariably set you apart. People will certainly relate with you the way they perceive you. Be very conscious of your appearance on every occasion and with every client. Beauty is attractive and above all adorable so, be pleasant, easy going and smart. Your appearance represents people's first impression about you. You need to have enough self-confidence to be objective.

There is need for decent, exquisite dressing, though in this field there is no such thing as dress rehearsal but dress in a way that depicts respect and be professional doing it. A wise man said you are addressed the way you dress. What am invariably cautioning here is to be simple, unique, modest and credible.

I have learnt from experience in business that everyone you meet deserves to be greeted with a smile. A good stance, direct eye contact, a firm handshake, welcoming look as well as excellent manners will send positive messages to your clients any day. Beyond this add some beauty tips to the business environment and display enthusiasm, energy, an outgoing and pleasant personality and a "can do" attitude. The potential of greatness is embedded in the acronym HDDPF - hard work, persistence, diligence, determination, focus and a little of other key things (good dress sense, neat office environment).

It is important to know how to manage your finance this is the constant inflow and outflow of money through your business at the most basic and important level.

Having the knowledge, skills and credentials to fulfil clients' expectations is the key in any business success. Event planning is no exception. You will need accounting skill for budgeting. You may have series of skills and an outstanding service you would want to offer clients, but choosing one or multiple area(s) you know best can help give you a clear advantage. Your versatility is what guarantees excellence.

After planning the event, the central function of management is controlling. Without the knowledge of project management, control becomes impossible. The control of an event can range from the event manager simply walking the site and discussing daily progress with staff, to implementing and monitoring a detailed plan of responsibilities, reports and budgets. Event planning can be effective only if the execution of the plan is carefully controlled. To do this it is necessary to develop proper control mechanisms.

Generally, events are characterized by two types of controls – operational and organizational. Operational controls are used for the day - to – day running of the event. Organizational controls relate to the overall objectives of the event organization, for example, whether the event is profitable and satisfies the client's brief.

Event control can be expensive in time and money. Its cost and effectiveness depend on the choice of the control mechanisms that make up the control system.

Control mechanism must be:

- Meaningful and efficient: Directed only at those areas that contribute to the success of the event.
- Simple: Controls must not be any more complicated than is necessary
- Relevant: Controls must be prepared to match each area of event management and should be distributed to those who have the responsibility of carrying them out.
- Timely and flexible: Deviation from plan should be identified early and addressed before they develop further. Flexibility is essential, as the controls may need to respond to revision of the event plan up until the last moment. Sometimes milestones or key dates must be moved to accommodate changes in the event. For example, a benchmark (identifiable points in the organization of the event where high standard is achieved) may be an attendance of 800guests and only 500 were accommodated at the chosen site, it is no longer a best practice benchmark and must be dropped in case it creates a logistical problem.
- Able to suggest actions: The most useful control mechanisms provide corrective actions to be taken when members of the event team find a gap between the plan and reality.

When deviations or gaps are identified, the Event planner can make a reasoned choice – either to the gap, or to leave it alone and revise the plan.

You should make it a duty to find out what paper work and recording is needed in the event industry.

Managing money cost and profit is very important to Event planners. There are a variety of resources available to help you keep track of your business income and expenses. Most appropriately be acquainted with:

- Costs (Estimated, actual, variability)
- Contingencies (weather, suppliers, etc.)
- Profit (cost, contingencies, and remainder)

Creating a budget

Financial intelligence is a must for every event professional.

A budget is a list of all planned expenses and revenues that is workable and realistic. It is a plan for saving, revenues and spending. In other words, it is an organizational plan stated in monetary terms. Budgeting is also a pricing tool that can be used for forecasting with exactness whether the event will result in a gain, a loss or will breakeven. The objective of creating a budget is to provide event planners with financial blueprint. It enables the actual financial operation of the event to be measured against forecast.

It's easy to throw caution to the wind and end up spending a great deal more than you intended. It might sound impractical to work on a budget before knowing venue and catering costs, but working this way provides a benchmark for you to measure all vendor proposals. Begin with your revenue sources. How much will you be charging participants? The budget of an event is used to compare actual costs and revenues with projected costs and revenues. That is the estimate of the cost and revenues of an event. Revenues will ultimately dictate your budget, so it makes sense to project them first. Budgets are important to event managers. A budget is based on reasonable projections made within an economic framework. Small changes in framework can cause large changes in the event's finances.

When developing a budget, marketing should be included where necessary. After you have identified your revenue sources, the next thing should be to outline your marketing plan. What is the best way to reach and engage your revenue generators?

According to Joe LoCicero, budget can be the one component that sends the project off course, mitigates its success, or stops it from taking flight to begin with. A budget must be implemented for an event small or large scale.

The event planner defines event budget by finding out how much the client is willing to expend and what will be the cost of producing, marketing and operating the event. By this I mean you must be able to recover your production, marketing and operating cost and a considerable profit if is a corporate event. For such, budget consists of cost, contingencies and profits.

The budget should be specific that means you break it down to each phase of the event using percentages where necessary, and it should include revenue opportunities if available whether is for 10 or 3000 people. Budget consist of cost (estimated and actual cost, plus contingency (weather, suppliers and plus and profit). Your job is to keep the actual cost at or below the estimated cost; to use as little of the design allowance (the money set aside in the budget "just in case" the actual cost of the item is widely different than the estimate and the contingency as possible and to maximize the profit to be earned. Cost cutting while important must balance with highest levels of service and satisfaction to clients.

Always ask clients how much they are willing to spend for their event so as to get your working plan very clear. In order to help client plan and allocate their budget, an estimated figure can be prepared to help decide how much money the client will expend on an event and how the money will be allocated to each activity. Such budgetary items may include entertainment, catering and venue fee.

If food is needed, whether it is a light luncheon, or a full dinner, you will need a caterer or budget for special plates and foods. If entertainment is needed or specialized speakers, you'll have to pay for their time. If favours are needed or souvenirs plan for what kind, how many and what they will be distributed in. Corporate gifts will require extra time and thought. The gifts may bear the company logo and be somewhat representative of the event or the company. Will there be transportation for client and guests? If it's a themed or costumed event you will need to budget for relevant props, setting and extra costume materials. If is red carpet event, you will need to provide red carpet, props and valet services, if location doesn't have one.

In budget preparation each of these costs is estimated and totalled.

As an event planner, it is very important you learn and know the differences between estimated cost and actual cost, budgeting and cost control and keeping of records. If this is beyond your company capacity, then get an account supervisor to help with your budgets and financial management.

Where we are today, is only good enough for the now, if we stay there too long sudden financial occurrences may catch up with us, we should build our businesses to a stage of getting the desired customers that can bring us the profit needed to run the business.

There is need for a dynamic strategy to be devised and a budgeting system adopted in your business. You should be able to get all details regarding contracted vendors documented.

As events differ, so will the budget line items needed for the event. Your budget may go into the following and more:

- Rentals
- Venue fees
- Entertainment
- Audio – visual needs
- Promotion, publicity and advertising
- Design and printing
- Administration

The planner must ascertain definitely your priorities or goals and may have to exclude certain items. Interview potential service providers to decide which is best for your event.

Steps to creating a budget

1. Identify the resources required for the event
2. Estimate the cost for each of those resources
3. Document the costs
4. Identify ways of covering the costs.

Scrutinize your actual costs as they emerge, and then compare and prioritize them to reach your projected goals. This tool is a dire necessity when overseeing financial project, and a precise budget is your most valuable resource for making intelligent choices.

Take time out to learn basic budgeting skills to check budget over runs and as well monitor the budget as event tasks progresses. Be sure to update your budget frequently.

Always put extras in your budget just in case something pops up.

Work with clients' budget, and get them involved at all stages of the event. Though cost cutting is important, you must balance this with a need to provide highest levels of service delivery and clients' satisfaction.

Estimates

An estimate is an educated guess regarding how much each required item would cost.

Sufficient information is needed for estimate to be accurate. When you add items to your budget, and then assign estimated cost to them. If you're in search of a venue that will accommodate 500 people, then ask for its availability by checking through some sites of that capacity. Bear in mind the date of event and compare prices. Be specific in designating cost estimates to each event category and be definite/ explicit.

Details such as:

     a.   Number of people expected
     b.   Date, time, and approximate length of event
     c.   Event purpose
     d.   What you need from service providers

Once estimate is made in all categories, add up the number and see if the proposed budget is proportionate with company's finances.

It is advisable to give estimate in advance for all services especially if you are taking charge of the whole event. This estimate must be written for the client whenever there is a need for it without delay. Billing clients should be based on actual labour and equipment to be used, but never let your billing exceed the estimate unless there are changes in the event needs in which case there will be need for additional labour and equipment. Underestimating can happen quite easily this makes it reasonable taking necessary precautions are taken.

If you are planning the event to break even, there are some possibilities to check out for additional source of income. Among these are:

    a.   Registration fees for the event
    b.   Ticket sales for admission to the event
    c.   Sales of advertisements
    d.   Merchandize sales such as books, T-shirts miscellaneous items
    e.   Booth space sales
    f.   Donated items that are auctioned off at the event.

Exchange and transactions

Exchange is the core concept of marketing; it involves obtaining a desired product or service from someone by offering something in return.   For exchange to take place, the event planner and clients have to agree on terms that will leave them both better off.

Selling skills therefore is required to find new clients.

Timely execution of event

Self - management starts with the commitment to change. This industry goes on every day that means planners work mornings, evenings, weekdays, weekend's holidays.   They are always organizing and running events that simply must go on, and go smoothly. Time management errors can cost a company a potential sale, lose them an existing customer, and damage their professional reputation.

It is essential that planners know how to manage their own time as well as they manage an event for smooth event implementation, and for business success. Engage team members on tasks that can train them to be more productive rather than been time wasters. Improve on time management through better planning, prioritizing, controlling your environment, understanding yourself and identifying what you will change about your habits, routine and attitude. The key to time management is planning and then protecting the planned time. If you plan what to do and when, and then stick to it, then you will have time. Self - management is chiefly about conditioning your environment, rather than allowing your environment to condition you.

Event planners must learn how to deal with the principles of personal management and personal organization if they are to remain relevant in business.

How can you effectively manage time as an event planner?

This is so crucial to event planning and execution of task. Otherwise, the event planner would end up wasting so much time doing relatively little and achieving unfruitful results.   Personal management is fundamental to job performance in event planning. The concept of personal management has been defined as the "efficient use of our resources, (people, materials and so on) in such a way that you are effective in achieving important personal and organizational goals".

It has to do with task duration for each event, dependencies and all critical paths. Events are broken into a number of tasks that have to be performed within specific deadlines.

To be efficient, you do the right things but to be effective you do the right things at the right time and do excellently.

Self - management is a critically important skill aimed at meeting deadlines. It is continuous, ongoing process of strategic planning, analysing, over–all monitoring, crisis management and re-planning. Keeping track of time can save you enough time and fatigue and good client relationship.

Event entertainers for instance that work many corporate and fundraising events should be able to present at the right time. There is nothing worse than the comedian going on when dinner is being served or half the audience is waiting for their meal and the other half is ready to get on with the "dance band"

There is need to analyse exactly what task you're spending time on, and how important are those tasks and portions of time to the successful completion of the event. From the planning phase of an event to budgeting, seeking vendors, and purchasing of event supplies time should be adequately utilized. Time is a valuable resource to planners and it affects the way other resources are utilized, there is need therefore to take absolute control of your time. Can you imagine a scenario where all the details of the event are taken care of, the RSVP are in, and it looks like your special event is going to have a huge crowd, but one of the most important things to make the afternoon really successful and memorable is still to be done.

For instance, is far too much a risk to the event planner to have staff without the pre-requisite knowledge on how handling events.

The critical path must be identified for effective self - management in establishing a music festival and other events.

Time is the only resource that all humans have equally. Time cannot be managed as you do with people, money and other physical assets. You need to know when to visit client, when to start planning and preparing, when to visit vendors, when to start and end any task. Time management is simply the self- management of all activities relating to the event production. The key to successful time management is planning and then protecting the planned time. Those who say they have no time, do not plan, or fail to protect the planned time. If you plan what to do, when to do it, and then stick to it, you will have enough time. An old adage says "time is money."

Never take your tasks for granted, give attention to little details and neglect time wasting activities. Managing your time involves conditioning, or re-conditioning your environment, to suit your plans. Time is limited, perishable, irretrievable, uncontrollable, irreplaceable and inelastic. We all have the same time advantage.

Preparation is the ideal word here, be prepared to handle any task without stress and having no slack time. Proper utilization of time for each event task is something you learn and adapt to overtime. Package yourself for every occasion that you are involved in planning. Synergy of purpose between your staff, vendors as well as volunteers if available needs to be inculcated from start.

Have one goal for every event knowing that all eyes are on you to do the underground work necessary to perform beyond the ordinary.

When you properly manage time as an event planner it will ensure everything is carefully cemented. Timely preparing an invoice for your clients will ensure credibility. Timing is everything for a planner; otherwise, you will never have enough of it to execute your project. Get self – help books on how to effectively control time. You must learn to plan and exercise conscious control of time spent on specific activities, especially to increase effectiveness, efficiency and productivity.

You don't want to end every event wishing you'd done something you didn't get to do would you? Never respond to pressures but to established priorities. Using relevant chart is important in this case, it typically shows the beginning and end dates for a project as well as tasks for accomplishing the project.

Controlling your time

Time is precious and must be judiciously managed pre-event, at event and post-event.

a. Analyse and prioritize tasks
b. Make a coordinated list of action plan. Things which matter most should not be at the expense of things that matter the least
c. Structure your workload and your day for maximum performance
d. Creatively attend to tasks by focusing on truly important activities and ignoring unimportant tasks
e. The important things even if they are not urgent activities, should come up before others
f. Know how to delegate, outsource and even partner with suppliers in crunch period
g. Never procrastinate; as Gary Feller said "one reason procrastinators seldom become creative: deadlines sneak up on them". There is an English proverb which says "don't put off until tomorrow what you can do today".
h. Identify when extra help is needed
i. Reduce stress producing time crunches.

Event Planners should also:

a. Find out how you can use time most productively when there is an event to manage.
b. ii. Set goals that are important to executing your planned event, by means of prioritizing your event tasks or activities based on their relative importance.
c. iii. Develop action plan to achieve important goals, resource needs and deadlines.

You can only prioritize the task you have judiciously noted down with deadlines. If you have a limited time to plan for an event and execute it, prioritizing every activity should be the bottom line. This means you are taking a good look at what has to be done and determining just what task must be done first.   You need to know when to visit client, when to start purchasing, when to arrive at the venue and when to end a task.   These little details will set you apart as an expert.   No information is too small to note, hence event planning calls for being organized and detailed.

Do not handle activity on a first come first serve basis. If you do, some problems may be covered until it is too late to handle. The solution is to sit back each evening or first thing each morning and see what you have on your desk for an event. Take the time to analyse everything critically and map out strategies. Thereafter, sort your work into piles and tackle the top priority jobs first, as this is done delegate responsibility and make every hour productive.

You must of necessity to devote time to each of your task.

Most event planners find it very difficult rationing their time. Rationing is very simple; it is looking at each task ahead of you for a day and deciding just how much time you will devote to it. Every program that does not contribute to your assignment should be eliminated.

If you have a policy which insists that you be constantly interrupted why not try reviewing the policy because this is a big-time management detractor in the world today. When you engage in irrelevant issues you stress yourself unnecessarily. Hence, managing stress is one way to effectively manage your personality.

Be prepared to make drastic changes and be creative to find and introduce different ways of doing things. Through personal management your integrity will far outshine your faults and you truly will become awesome.

Delegation

Delegation is entrusting part of your assignment to those you trust can get it done. It also makes division of labour or task allocation easy that is assigning to others what they are good at doing. It creates authority, responsibility and objectives for results. It therefore means that building trust is a plus to service delivery.

The job of an Event planner is basically that of delegating, this is what enables you manage any event successfully and get best result. Division of work is primarily aimed at ensuring specific responsibilities are assigned to individuals or teams in order to achieve goals and objectives. In this process, individuals are assigned jobs related to their area of specialty. It is not possible to provide every service required for an event all by yourself.

There is need for a management structure that determines relationships between functions and positions. This means you delegate roles, responsibilities and authority to execute defined tasks. Without delegation, event task becomes almost impossible. Delegation is a managerial function which must be used to its advantage by event planners who want to succeed. Learn what to delegate, what to delete or unload and what not to include in the first place. You have the same twenty – four hours to respond to either pressure or priorities.

The technique to use encompass the following:

- Decide which work your staff, service providers and others will handle.
- Delegating authority to others will help you manage effectively; you are not a dead sea always gathering and never giving out. Delegation will bring the following:
  a. Concentration and efficiency
  b. You will be able to come up with something more unique
  c. Decision will be made at the lowest possible time
  d. It provides a good way of training subordinate
  e. It brings relief

Requirement for delegation

One major pre-requisite I have noticed while delegating is trust. Have faith in those around you and in your team. Never be suspicious of them or feel insecure by their presence. Everyman great or small has great potentials, so don't look down on your employees whether regular or contract staff.

Departmentalize your business and engage employees thus.

Give opportunity to people to exercise themselves. Correct mistakes made and give them time to change. Every perfect man has made a mistake at one time or the other and such errors or mistakes have made their best to manifest.

Encourage initiative

Give people opportunity to come up with suggestions and give assignments that will help them do better. If you do not give room for this, the purpose for delegating is defeated. Be honest and realistic with your employees, allow your team to develop mentally and reason properly with less instruction.

Nature is not unaware of the essence of time; hence day and night were created by God. And the day and night were again fractionized into seconds, minutes, hours. The same day and night were accumulated into weeks, months and years. This arrangement is predicted on the quest for time management.

Until you get into action, you are merely a fan of your dreams. There is working time for event planners. Don't just plan but execute your plans using your time conceptually. If you invest your time wisely and adequately you cannot but be a star on earth.

Avoid whatever is a time waster by challenging it whether habitual tasks or meetings. Think about why you are doing things, and the best way to get them done.

There is danger in the comfort zone. This is the zone where you think everything comes so naturally and effortlessly without keeping abreast of diligence.

It is a place where no one can touch you. Being in your comfort zone makes you a master of your own house and your own craft.

At no time should you be complacent with your service delivery. Complacency can be big problem for event planners that have been in business for more than a few years.

The danger is becoming so relaxed in what you do and what you know, that any kind of change in your daily routine becomes frightening, and that limits you from exploiting your total potential and getting the most of your work day. Determine how far you want to go with the business, how you will best serve your clients.   Be a goal getter, curious and daring.   Above all be prepared to break the status quo.

Chapter Thirteen

Event evaluation

Businesses spend quite a huge sum of money organizing meetings and events each year. However, organizations rarely measure the impact of meetings and events, what did attendance at meetings or events change in the performance of individuals and organization as a whole. Event evaluation appraises the progress and performance of an event and compares it to what was originally planned.

Good Management of events can give you a competitive advantage especially in event development.

In order to learn, people require feedback, like that gained by a team from reviewing game films.

The last phase of an event should be a final process review, conducted so the management of event can be improved.

However, such a process review should not be conducted only at the end of the event. Rather, process reviews should be done at major milestones in the project or every three months, so that learning can take place as the job progresses.

Two questions should be asked in the review. The first is "what have we done so well so far?" and the second is "what do we want to improve (or do better) in the Future?"

Event evaluation is necessary to make the planner and team members more effective and efficient. Event evaluation appraises the progress and performance of an event and compares it to what was originally planned. It is about identifying mistakes and learning from such mistakes. It is normally a meeting with team members which should come up immediately at the end of an event.

Answering the key Questions

There is an approach to evaluate events and conferences that provides answers to the following key Questions as suggested by Glenn O'Neil

a. What did participants appreciate and values of the event?
b. What were the main strengths and weaknesses of the event?
c. Did the event meet its overall objectives or not?
d. Did the event lead to changes in the way participants do their work now or in the future?
e. How can the event be improved in the future?

Measuring quality and value

Through interaction with event participants, an assessment of the following aspects of the event has been undertaken:

a. Quality and relevance of speakers/moderators
b. Quality and relevance of topics/themes addressed
c. Preference and rating of event for mats (e.g. workshops versus plenary sessions)
d. Performance of services for participants (e.g. registration, venues, catering)

These aspects are rated and ranked by participants into key benefits and areas to be improved. See figure 13.1.

1. High quality factors; networking, social events, and administration.
2. Greatest benefits of attending
3. Factors to be improved; auditorium catering websites, discussions

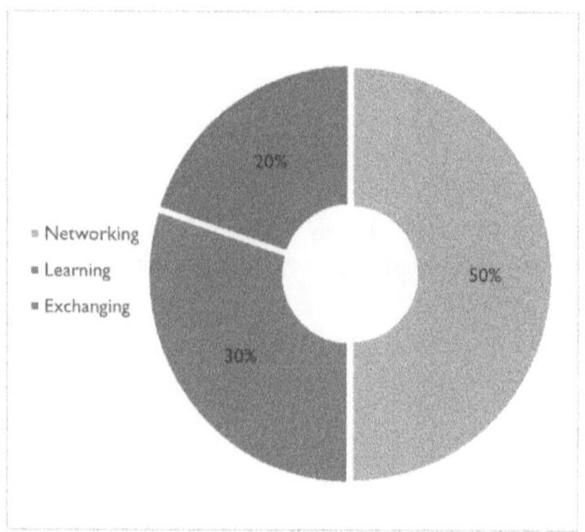

figure 13.1: Measuring Quality and Value

Accomplishing event objectives

A key question often asked by event organizers is; "did we accomplish our objectives?"

Through interaction with participants, we can determine to what extent event objectives have been accomplished through interaction with participants.

Objectives achieved

The objectives to be achieved include; connecting people, providing information on emerging technologies, and influencing opinions on emerging technologies. The graph below presents the objectives in a ranked funnel by priority.

Connect people, 96%

Provide Information on Emerging Technologies, 86%

Influence Opinions on Emerging Technologies, 73%

Assessing the longer-term impact of events organization increasingly want to know what is the long-term impact of events. How much did the event influence the way people work? This can be done by caring out a follow-up surveys and interviews with participants to determine what and how event has impacted their work in areas including

1. Changes to the way the find information?
2. Changes to the way they do certain tasks?
3. Growth of their professional network?
4. Initiation of new activities?

Measuring the impact of meetings and events is very important, what did attendance at meetings or events change in the performance of individuals and organizations as a whole?

The quality and value of the event also need to be measured, so as to know factors that must be improved on when another event is held. Was the objective achieved?

The longer-term impact should also be assessed-how did the event influence the way people work?

Measuring the impact of meetings and events is very important; what did attendance at the event change in the performance of individuals and organizations as a whole? The quality and value of the event also need to be measured, so as to know factors that must be improved on when another event is held.

A key question to be asked by planner is "did we accomplish our objectives?" The longer-term impact should also be assessed – how did the event influence the way people work? Then, how can the event be improved in the future?

Good management of events gives a competitive advantage especially in event development. In order to learn, people require feedback. The last phase of an event should be a final process review, conducted so the management of event can be improved.

Continually evaluate on the purpose of the project at hand to remain relevant in an ever-changing world.

Complimentary services for event evaluation include Return on investment ROI) calculations, network mapping, media/online monitoring (event visibility) and panel studies. There should be a cost – effective evaluation.

Chapter Fourteen

Setting up your event planning business

Starting an event planning business doesn't require much. You can really start-up   from scratch with not too much of capital except you are considering renting an office space. What you need is, training, experience, startup research and right contact. Having a sense of business savvy is crucial.

Having done all the startup research, you will be ready to make a few decisions based on your findings. Think carefully about your needs and feel free to try out a variety of scenarios until you settle into something you think will work best for you.

It will certainly take time to get known and find clients but ensure you are determined. You must be prepared for this because if you don't have clients, you have nothing to be creative about.

Have a full knowledge of your business and the message you are conveying. Know the benefit of your message, its uniqueness and have evidence. These are your unique selling proposition.

Your clients will expect the most organized event for their money. Being able to negotiate prices for services, supplies, and venue rent is essential to save money. Saving money will increase your profit margin, as well as allow you to outbid other event planners in your area.

Research

There should be adequate preparation.

Preparation is the starting point of any business. If you are not duly prepared, you may have to rethink starting your own business otherwise you will get shut mid-way. Doing a survey in the town or city where you will be doing business will help you pitch your tent successfully. Researching the market is a way of finding out early the target market is. If you need to go into meeting planning and only two meetings are held every six months, then selling that type of service is not commercially viable.

The major things I have noticed Event planners spend the bulk of their time in, is trying to find new clients, writing proposals and convincing someone to hire them. This involves thinking and creating guidelines for efficiency.

Game plan

Design your game plan with these fail-proof questions;

j.   What segment (client and event) will my market be?
a.   Are there segments which I will not pursue?
b.   What are my personality strengths?
c.   What are my experiences and what did I learn?
d.   What are my business skills?
e.   What is my education/ training as it pertains to event planning industry?
f.   What are my areas of expertise I will do myself?
g.   Who are established contacts, including vendors?

Have a vision

Besides having mission statements to communicate who you are and what you do, you should also have vision statements to describe your ultimate achievements.

Throughout history the greatest leaders were "seers" that is somebody who can see beyond what everybody else was looking at. You can see what is down the road and you can see what it is going to take to get there. Visionaries are people who are not satisfied with what is happening but who are interested in what's going to happen and how they can make it happen. The vision or guiding purpose is the source from which leadership derives its magnetic field to activate the commitment, cooperation and confidence of others. There is no one that is born without a definite purpose in life. A vision must be healthy and must be grasped not only by business owners or leaders, but the followers or employees as well. Therefore, a major responsibility of a leader is to accurately and effectively communicate his vision to the group. Both then commit to act on the vision, and then proceed to design goals program to achieve the mission and thus fulfil the vision. The commitment includes a determination to overcome difficulties and eliminate obstacles. Make a clear and strong decision on how you can make your services worthwhile.

Vision is a comprehensive sense of where you are, where you are going and how you intend getting there.

Have a mission statement

This is simply the legitimate purpose of the existence of the business to the society at large. Get it stated down appropriately and clearly.

Describe what your company does. It might be helpful to focus on your business's core competencies when you are considering which values are worthy of being a part of your mission statement. Once you have decided which core values are most important, add one (or two at most) to the service description of what your company does. When you write a mission statement, this is the part that describes your spark, or the passion behind your business.

Why does your business do what it does? For some people, it helps to think back on why they started their business in the first place.

Besides your mission statement directing your business planning, you want your mission statement to be front and centre in the minds of everyone who works in your business and communicated to customers and/or clients. As the statement of why you exist, it's also the statement that explains to them why they would want to do business with you. Some businesses go as far as to make their mission statements the themes of their advertising campaigns. If you do nothing else, you should make sure your mission statement is highly visible in your business premises, on your website if you have one, and on all your marketing materials.

Have goals and objectives

Successful people are goal oriented, thorough and decisive. They have enough self-confidence to be objective. Goals can be defined as the prophecies of what you shall one day become. Goals are the single most important factor in achieving success. All successful people constantly set goals, re-evaluate their goals and scale them upward toward even greater accomplishment. The purpose of goals is to focus our attention. The mind will not reach towards achievement until it has clear objectives. Goal setting gives focus, orderliness and a reason to hope for a better future. A set goal minimizes unnecessary busy works that leads to nowhere. Having goals give one the guts to be determined, believe in a worthy pursued idea, it extinguishes fear, doubt, procrastination and unnecessary excuses and become more action-oriented.

You need unflinching purpose and determination, clear-cut goals and plans which you can adhere strictly to. Lack of purpose and direction can destroy your business. When you lack definite goals, you experience little or no growth.

How do you work out your goals?

a. Prioritize your goal
b. Set a definite date and time to undertake a specific task
c. Take action on a thing at a time
d. Observe what's working and what's not working and take note
e. Direct your focus to areas to areas that need improvement.

Objectives represent the desired outcome that you hope to attain eventually in the course of managing the business. They are more specific than mission and vision, and often include time schedule for completion. Objectives will serve as standard and as motivator. Your objectives should be visualized. Visualization uses the power of imagination. Focusing becomes extremely important here. If you don't have a vision for your business then you haven't probably focused in on anything.

There is need for to have short term, medium term and long-term objectives.

Service description

A good description of the type of services you will be providing and how you will get at it is vital.

Acknowledge what you want to do to maintain a positive mindset, energy level and positive space to do what you love.

Most likely, you will need to hire service providers. Identify them here at least by occupation. If you know by name who you want to work with, include that information also. You will probably outsource printers, graphic artists, caterers and bakers etc. You should do some research to find out the service provider that puts up the best work for the best price. The quality of their work will reflect on you. Always keep a job schedule as well as a checklist, every great man has his schedules.

The central point of it all is to get relevant professional knowledge. Adequately study the basics of the business and have all required facts about it at your fingertips. Know who is who in the industry. It is a business that requires you to set goals and make relevant plans.

Developing an effective business plan

It is valuable to have a robust planning tool that will help you think through your business systematically. It has to do with putting all the plans for your business on paper. This is a summary written of an entrepreneur's proposed business venture, its operational and financial details, its marketing opportunities and strategy, and its skills and experience. A business plan describes the direction the company is taking, what its goals are, where it wants to be, and how it's going to get there. The plan is written proof that you have performed the necessary research, has studied the business opportunity adequately, and is prepared to capitalize on it with a sound business model. A business plan can be a single page depending on if you will be needing loan from the bank or not. Part of any business plan is laying out your business.

One of key objectives of the business plan is show to the potential investors that the new business has a sound business model and a venture will be able to repay loans and produce an attractive rate of return. But even if you will not be needing loan you still need to have things in its proper perspective. What is your business about? Define it specifically in your business plan. Let go of jobs that are not what your business is about and focus on what you are supposed to do.

In preparing your business plan you deal with the details of how you're practically going to realize the vision. This means you have to decide on how to provide your services, persuade customers, respond to your competitors, find and keep good people and even decide how to pay yourself. A marketing plan is also incorporated into your business plan. Planning and operation should be customer oriented and activities marketed to meet customers need.

If you intend to seek outside financing which is not too relevant in this business, the financier will require a detailed business plan to show you're serious about your ideas. The purpose is to convince your financier that your ideas and approach are viable and that you have strong chance(s) for success.

Even if you don't need external financial aid, putting ideas on paper will give you a blueprint of where you're going with your business and how you are going to get there.

Developing a business plan involves putting all plans for your business on paper and it includes:

    h.   Identifying your startup cost
    1.   Determining your strategy for getting clients

2. Understanding what obstacles, you may be up against
3. Focusing on what services you intend to offer and how to market same.
4. How do you propose to reach clients?
5. What kind of image do you want to convey to customers?
6. Managing the business itself
7. Who are your competitors?

Have a robust marketing plan as shown in an earlier chapter. Thoroughly describe all of the services that you offer as well as the price of each service. Discuss whether all of these services are offered as a package or whether individual services can be put together for custom pricing. Also discuss any additional features you offer to clients.

Know your target audience

This becomes very possible when you have done major research into the market. There are strategies you must employ before you kick start your business and one of such as earlier discussed is finding a niche and knowing your target audience. You must be able to define your target clearly and concisely. Find out the niche markets that exist in your area, what their needs may be; where they live, their age range, their general desire and who their event planner is presently. Design a specialized service for a part of the market that you find interesting. This is because many people actually need the services of event planners and this includes organizations that use events to call attention to their products.

The entrant must of necessity research and discover who her services are likely to benefit the most. Researching can also give you great inspiration for future event plans depending on which aspect of event planning you are focusing on. The planner's business may never be able to solve event problems as it relates to everybody in the community therefore, she should figure out which segment(s) of the community are not being reached by competitors that she can take advantage of reaching with her business.

Being in your strength zone will make things work out naturally. Targeting is the fitting strategy of any company. Your event planning outfit needs to select the market segment that has "good" size to generate expected financial returns.

Find out questions that relate to:

- What do they really want?
- What style of marketing best matches the target?
- Which people among the segment is your business designed to reach?
- What is their taste and style? Getting to know the taste and style of potential clients is also important. Once you have determined client's taste and need, you then map out strategies for providing the service.

Every event planning business should be able to reflect client's lifestyle, and meet their expectations; clients want to be comfortable and relaxed on the event day and not under stress. Then choose a format that reaches that segment. The world is filled with target markets just waiting for you to provide a specialty service to fill a need.

Know the purpose why you are communicating to any group. Is it for entertainment, wedding, parties or why?

- What is it you want to do for the particular client?
- When is the right time to get it done?

Having an operational plan that answers the above questions will enhance productivity, and bring out your unique selling point.

To judiciously do this, you must:

- Understand the customer
- Know how the client perceives your business
- Deliver quality and value

By considering a target market, you are familiar with in expertise, you are better able to determine realistic needs that can be met by your services.

Satisfaction in business generates loyalty, so that in any decision regarding where to get an event planner, your business comes to mind. A truly successful event planner is one which will provide services able to satisfy all of customers need. Increasing efficiency in delivery of services will boost business capacity. Your capacity refers to how much your business can produce during a specific period of time. Clients will flock around you for efficiency, satisfaction of needs, exclusiveness and uniqueness of service.

You may need to remember the following:

- The bigger the market size the more lucrative the segment to your company.
- Use competitive advantage to measure whether your company has such strength and expertise to dominate the chosen market segment. You will also have to build a sustainable competitive advantage over competitors.

Consider the competition intensity within the industry in your community including number of players, vendors, suppliers as well as entry barrier.

Examples of target market for planners include individuals, businesses, families and government entities.

It is penitent to also position your firm rightly. Positioning is met to satisfy your customers credibly, this is about being trustworthy, confident and competent towards reaching the target you have chosen creatively.

If your company has gotten the necessary elements, customers will then have the "being" of your company within them. Positioning is to earn customers' trust and make them willing to follow you. Positioning is the reason for being. This will in turn make customers come to see your firm in that light. Be an expert in your community and plan your business around the purpose of the organization. You certainly need to schedule your purpose on your calendar, otherwise it won't get emphasized.

Differentiation is also important to your target market. This is the result of efforts to make your business stand out as a provider of unique value to your customers in comparison with its competitors. This is an industry getting saturated and you must differentiate your offerings.

You become the cynosure of all eyes when you discover the right audience that best suite you and satisfy them. "The secret to success is to know something nobody else knows and to do what no one knows how to do.

Steps to getting clients

Questions to ask include:

a. Why do clients come to me to organize their events?
b. What do I really do for my clients?
c. What makes me better than my competitors?
d. What special skills do I have?
e. How can I improve on my weaknesses?

The answers to these questions are your competitive advantage. They make you better off.

- Learn to create useful message that attracts easily
- Use positive language to gain client's trust
- Deliver your message as often as your budget allows.

People choose event planners primarily on the basis of relationship and essential programs.

When you do what customers can't find anywhere closer to them, they run after you. Every business has a unique fishing pond and each pond is stocked with a different number and types of fish.

Look at every successful event planner and you will discover a common denominator; they have figured out a way to meet the real needs of people. A business will never grow beyond its capacity to meet needs.

Choose a winning business name

When choosing a business name, there are two things to consider, the business name's marketing potential and its legal elements. The business name registration is a legal requirement for almost all business in Nigeria.

Legal matters

All of the following are commonly required to start a new business:

- Choose a creative business name, not copying others and get properly registered with the corporate affairs commission or the right organization. When choosing a name consider its legal elements and marketing potentials do not go for names that are difficult to pronounce. Every land has its law and ignorance of the law is no excuse.
- Choose a business legal structure (sole proprietorship, Partnership etc).

Sole proprietorship

If you want to run the business yourself, without incorporating, your business will be known as a "sole proprietorship. This is the least expensive way to start an event planning business and it leaves you taking all decisions for the business alone. It is also easiest because it requires less paperwork and you can report your business income on your personal accounting package.

The downside includes the lack of financial protection

- Since you are your company, all your personal assets are subject to the ups and downs of your business. That means you are personally liable for any debts the business incurs, as well as managing risk involved in the course of running the business.

Partnership

A partnership works like a sole proprietorship except that the risks are split between two or more people. One person may have more of a percentage of the business, or it may be equally shared. Legally, you would all be responsible for any debts. The best advice is to spend many hours talking about how everything fits together before you jump into it and get it legally sealed.

Issues to clearly define include:

- What will each of you be responsible for?
- How will you make decisions on a day-to-day basis?
- What percentage of the business will each party own?
- How do you see the business developing in the future?
- What do you expect from each other?

Ensure you get an agreement that legally binds the parties involved otherwise there maybe conflict of interest as the business grows.

Tag lines

You might also want to include what's called a 'tag line' or 'Slug Line' after your company name. Tag lines or call it slogan can create brand awareness of their own. Lots of companies use a tag line to make up for an otherwise non-descript name.

Your company name and what comes after it help you stand apart from your competition. Give this the time and consideration it deserves and get registered with the necessary organization and never clog into using already existing business names and tags.

Company colour

Once you have decided on a name you should determine your company colours. When choosing colours, bear in mind how and where you will use them.

Possibilities Include:

a.   Office Décor

b.   Company Vehicles if available

c.   Collateral materials and marketing pieces and more.

Developing your logo

Unless you have skills and feel up to the task designing an image yourself, you should consider contracting a designer to create a unique logo that best suit your business image.

Getting a work space

Consider where you are going to do your business. Are you starting from home or getting an office. Whichever of the two choices make your workplace decent and the atmosphere welcoming as well as inviting

Being an effective organizer means doing all you are paid to do and much more. In event planning there are numerous details to be handled.

The truth is, no matter how good you are in many tasks and how multi-talented you are, get others involved. The more unique your service is, the easier it is to convince clients to turn their events to you.

It is also important to add some beauty tips to your business environment.

Dedication

Every successful event planner is dedicated to duty.

This has to do with working hard at your job. I also see it as faithful commitment to purpose.

Many people get into event planning business without a true understanding of the time and energy required to be successful. Though event planning involves parties, fun and excitement, it also requires long hours of hard work. In spite of the fact that executing an event can be hard, physical work, your preparation to tackle managerial task makes the difference. As a beginner you may have some budget constraints and labour issues that demand you do most jobs alone. Whatever it is, be committed to making it worthwhile. Commitment to continuous personal improvement is the job security you have. Be a value driven person.

Dedication with patience is very important because most jobs are really stressful and strenuous. This is why been able to work calmly is a necessary pre-requisite. The principle of persistence is to act continuously not minding the prevailing circumstances. Is what not happening to you that matters but what you do to become professionally relevant.

Communication inventory

There is need to have an inventory of all communication tools and printed documents that will be utilized by your organization. Note the materials, purpose, how to distribute the materials and uses.

Materials you may want to include among others are:

- Business card
- Letterhead
- Envelope
- Invoices
- Stationery etc.

Meeting clients need

Finding new clients and keeping old ones is the most crucial task of Event planners. Customers don't expect to get bottom -of -the -barrel prices everywhere they go, but they do expect to be treated with respect.

Understanding customer needs is not always simple. Always be positive when meeting with a client. A responsive event planner finds a stated need and fills it. An anticipative Event planner looks ahead into what needs the customers may have in the near future.   A creative planner discovers and produces solutions customers did not ask for but to which they enthusiastically respond.

Satisfying target customers is supremely important because the business sales each period come from new customers and repeat customers. Learn to over deliver on your first customer contact. Give them something more than you promised, give a related service for free, go the extra mile. Be a solution to their problems especially when you have customers who have needs, they are not fully conscious of or they cannot articulate these needs or they use some words that require some interpretation.   This will help in putting your business right. Now you know who your target is in business. But you still must answer these questions:

- Are you going to be generic?
- Where are they located and how will you reach them?
- What does it mean when a client asks for an exquisite but inexpensive banquet or cocktail for 200guests?

Great customer service doesn't just happen it starts with employees who have been trained in the science of service. Ushers for instance, will treat guests as they have been treated by the planner. Treat employees in a respectful and caring manner and that will be transferred to customers. Happy employees make happy customers. Get employees to know who is hosting the event being organized and ensure they are well taken care of.

It is always relevant to refer to past experiences that are similar to client's event; this will help you gain more confidence.

Empower and motivate your customers, your suppliers and so on. The purpose of a business is to keep a customer. If a business successfully creates and keeps customers in a cost-effective way, it will make a profit while continuing to survive and thrive. We must also understand that customer retention is more important than customer attraction; this is so because one estimates that attracting a new customer can cost five times as much as pleasing an existing one.

Business fails when there is lack of sales. And of course, this refers to initial sales and resale. You are to first and foremost create and keep customers and to increase your value you need to build your customer base.

In developing a successful customer base two things to keep in mind are positioning and differentiation. Positioning is the way customers think and talk about your company when you are not there. Your position determines whether or not your customers buy, whether he buys again and whether he refers others to you. Everything you do with regards to your customer affects the way your customer thinks about you.

Differentiation refers to your ability to separate yourself and your product or service from that of your competitors. It is the key to building and maintaining competitive advantage. This is the advantage that your business has over your competitors in the same marketplace.

Emphasize to your customers that the special features and benefits you offer are so important that they should not even think of going somewhere else.

Sustaining your business

Explore circumstances that can boost your firm's success. They include untapped niches, weak competitors, client referrals, networking and publicity activities. Don't limit your imagination; consider all possibilities and opportunities.

After identifying the right clients, you may need to:

Always give practical, clear and concrete action steps that explain how you intend to fulfil your purpose. Offer a detailed plan for implementing your purpose.

Plan programs, schedule events, hire competent staff for each job, and know you can never do it all alone. These are specifics that people care about. Remember, nothing becomes dynamic until it is specific. The more specific your business vision is, the more it will gain attention and attract commitment. Quality and expertise will attract great number of patronages.

Ask confidently for big commitment. People want to be committed to something that gives significance to their lives. They respond to responsibilities that give life meaning and are attracted by a challenging vision.

Strategy to employ

1. Information seeking
   - Personally seek information on clients, vendors and competitors.

2. Persistency
   - Take repeated or different action to overcome obstacle.
   - Make personal sacrifice to complete job.

3. Demand for efficiency
   - Do things that exceed existing standards of excellence or always improve on past performance.
   - Strive to do things better, faster or cheaper.

4. Risk taking
   - Take moderate risks
   - Make preference for situation that involves moderate risk

5. Planning
   - Always set goals for each event
   - Set clear and specific short – term objectives
   - Set clear long – term objectives for business. Use logical step by step plans to reach goals
   - Evaluate alternatives

- Monitor progress and switch to alternative strategies when necessary to achieve desired goals.

6. Strength
- Persuasion and Networking
- Personal contact and telephone

7. Confidence
- Have strong belief in self and abilities
- Express confidence in own ability to complete task or meet challenges.

Strategies that will help you to be more professional are:

- Build expertise: Don't let your knowledge and skills get outdated. Make a commitment to build expertise and stay up to date with your industry
- Develop your emotional intelligence
- Honour your commitments. Whenever you make a promise to a client keep it. If it looks as if you won't be able to meet a deadline let your team or clients know as soon as sensibly possible.

However, do what you can to avoid ending up in this situation.

- Don't make excuses – Instead focus on meeting expectations as best you can, and on making the situation right.
- Be polite
- Have the tools you need. Do you show up to a client meeting lacking important samples? This requires advance planning, timeless and attention.

Focus on improving your time management and planning skills so that you're always in control.

Apply the SWOT analysis to know your strength, weaknesses. Opportunities

and threat to business success.

Critical success factors

    a.   Excellent communication system
    b.   Proper and systematic advertisement
    c.   Good social contacts

Marketing your business

A key component part of your business as I said before will be deciding what services your business will offer, and who you will offer them to.

Don't be shy about promoting your business to complete strangers after all every customer begins as a complete stranger.

Make sure your marketing is hitting the right buttons, don't by pass your audience needs. Make sure your social program is rich and that you integrate with as many social networks as possible. Many people remember events just for the after parties so make sure your parties are memorable. You need the right words to describe what you do: On your website, blogs, advertising copy, anything that your ideal client might read.

As a beginner these are ways to get noticed:

Portfolio

It shows examples of your work

- Photographs at event
- Testimonial letters from clients
- Brochures
- Anything else that shows your skill

Advertisement

Advertising is any paid form of non- personal presentation and promotion of goods and services by an identified sponsor. However, depending on the services you offer as an event planner and your targeted market, newspaper, radio and possibly even television advertising may benefit your marketing plan. Keep in mind that this is expensive and is often a shot in the dark. In doing this be mindful of the fact that you have a target audience and you are not serving the whole community.

Refresh old advertisements to attract new clients. Stretch out your view of potential clients. Your businesslike manner and dress sense, the company's stationery, all communicate something positive or negative to your clients.

If someone does not like a particular event or the organizer, there is no amount of advertisement that can change the persons, mind.

Design a website

This could be an interesting way to sell your business on line. Internet advertising is important.

Event hosting

Hosting events is important to event planners.

- What kind of event can you host for your company and for others?
- Find out and do it lavishly for best result.

Write columns

I started off by writing a column for a newspaper. You can check with your local newspapers or business journals and event related magazines to see if they may be interested in your idea. Press release is important to planners.

Engage in public relation

It is appropriate to develop a PR strategy by outlining objectives, targeted audience, key message and desired results that map back to objectives. Public relation simply means managing relations with one's public. By the word "public," I mean a group of people who are important to the well-being of your business. These include the customers, employees and the local communities. The ultimate goal of any PR is for a corporation, institution, organization or individual to win favour with the general public. Since public relation is using effective communication and persuasive skills to achieve a goal or goals that are necessary for image building, you should make sure your marketing is hitting the right audience needs.

By familiarizing yourself with the basics of public relations, you will be better prepared to launch an effective campaign, whether the goal is to increase business, spread goodwill, and reflect a positive image or further charity effort.

Be a speaker

People are attracted to special events and event planners should take advantage of this great opportunity. They want to see you exude that professional image. Therefore, offer to give presentations to local groups, service clubs or business organizations. The speech you are giving should be concise, entertaining and well-articulated. You may be asked to speak at a college or school functions, before a group or club, or at any number of events. Try everything possible to be professional.

Promotional marketing

The reason a great event planner defines the guest list and potential audience is primarily to target the marketing and promotion efforts to the intended audience.

Ensure that 45 – 60% of the people attending the event are targets of the product to be promoted and also have a fore knowledge of the promotional materials you will be using for any such event.

Promotional marketing is important in today's competitive market place; it is used to deliver information about your business. Promotional tools are working for an increasing number of companies looking for creative, cost-effective way to attract customers and prospective clients. If you are in this business, never ignore the power and incredible value of this often overlooked and underutilized tool. People may not show up at your event for two reasons either they are not interested or they don't know about the event. If someone doesn't like a particular band, there's no amount of advertising budget to change that person's mind, the same apply to whomsoever is organizing the event. Creating an event that people are interested in is easier to sell.

Examples of promotional products are decorative items imprinted with a company Logo, name or message, business gift items, incentives, stickers and newsletters. These products are used to build identity; influence prospects, advertise, support and strengthen other marketing efforts. Develop a cohesive set of promotional pieces when the resource is available. You can do a lot to promote your business.

Word of mouth

As with all industries, word of mouth is the key. It is the best way to market your services. It is only promotional method that is of clients, by clients and for clients. Encourage satisfied client to refer friends to your business.

I will make bold to say that in this digital age the best way to grow fast is through words of mouth which includes online social networks too. Twitter and face book pages should form part of your portfolio of marketing effort. You can also run successful events.

There are a number of functions where people ask others for recommendation for an event planner. In such cases the recommender has potentially benefitted the event planner and the service seeker. All you need is enough of the rumours of your perfect services to spread around and your business will begin to attract people no other advert medium could possibly have reached.

Negative words of mouth on the other hand can be devastating to your business as against positive word of mouth. Dissatisfied customers have a way of infecting others with a strong, negative predisposition toward your services. They are more likely to tell others about their bad experiences than satisfied customers are likely to relate good experiences.

Many have discovered that opinion of friends and families are far more persuasive than advertisement. When you are doing great, satisfied customers become your walking, talking billboard and mind you it is cost free. All you need is good customer relationship and quality service that comes from absolute positioning and the news about you will be all over the city.

Remember that customers need someone who can confidently handle their money, tell them the truth and make them happy and stress free in the long run.

To get customer referral

- Talk to your customer

Have real person – to – person conversations with as many customers relative to your employees, then you will need to prioritize. Find ways to have real, meaningful and ongoing conversations with them. This might mean inviting some to lunch.

- Serve their needs

Everything you do in your customer referral effort needs to be useful from your customer's perspective. Educate them while you engage them.

Networking

Networking is consistently meeting new people and making new friends, sharing ideas and having lots of fun. To network is to make active effort to know and talk to people, and let them know your interest in getting their job perfectly executed. It is the key to getting that first job and subsequent jobs in the event industry and at the same time the reason while business events are so enriching and fulfilling. Opportunity to network is all around you and is a great way to give an opportunity to establish business relationship. How much of it you do is up to you, never underestimate it.

A wide variety of people make up your network. They include, friends at work, past co-workers, old school mates, neighbours, relatives, people you have done business with, fellow club members, church members etc. Those with whom you network can either be prospective clients, or anyone who could refer you to clients.

In networking confidence and knowing the reason you do business is key. What benefits does your business have for clients? Talk more on that and neglect the features for ones.

Every business has its unique selling point and this actually is your competitive advantage. People at networking events want to know your unique proposition. What would your business do for their business or their friends?

It is a good idea to put some effort into expanding your collection of contacts all the time and also earn great money. Having made the contact, make sure the link is maintained. Networking will ensure you identify new business development opportunities, learn new approaches to confronting challenges, establish lasting friendship and promote yourself by speaking knowledgeably about the job.

When you network you give and you receive. Speed networking sessions are a great way to give an opportunity to guests to do business and make their suffered investment worth the penny.

Volunteering

Many planners have found out that working for an established company as volunteers or employee after training is a good way to learn the basics without taking on the extra headaches and risks of starting an outfit. On the other hand, an opportunity for independence inspires many people to want to be event planners.

Volunteering therefore is one best way of marketing yourself as entrant and it means offering your services without being paid or forced to do it. Up until recently, event planning was done through volunteering and committees with only a few paid positions. Volunteering is most important when you are interested in acquiring more skills. Assist in planning for a charity event. Nearly every event in existence needs volunteers and this is the best single way to get your foot in the door and get some experience.

Volunteering will give you a chance to see if you really enjoy the job because the perception of event planning is very different than the reality. "You need grace under pressure". Concentrate your volunteer on the type of events you'd like to plan. If you decide to volunteer make sure you are not an invisible volunteer, one of the masses. Make sure you are assisting the person in charge and that you get experience with a large variety of tasks.

It does not reduce your esteem to volunteer your service but rather it improves your confidence in the job. I believe you get things done easier when you have more confidence in yourself and on the job.

Prepare collateral materials

Always be prepared to hand out brochures to people. It's important you think through all the materials you might be using in the future to effectively market your business.

The most important thing to envisage all of the time is consistency and cohesiveness. All the pieces must look like they belong together and be presented in orderly fashion.

Spend time getting the basics together and keep a good supply of such materials at hand so that you can easily prepare proposals and dash off to a client's office at a moment's notice.

Required materials may include:

    a.   Certificate
    b.   An Introductory letter
    c.   A nice pocket folder with space for your business card.
    d.   Recommendations or referrals
    e.   A list of your services
    f.   A one – page synopsis of each theme event you can create.

g. Copies of pictures from events you have coordinated on a separate portfolio.

Don't be shy about promoting your business to complete strangers after all every customer begins as a complete stranger. Testimonials are good marketing tools; they are statement from your customers saying how great your business is. You can make it a standard procedure to ask your clients for testimonials whenever you are done with an event.

The things you are looking for in a testimonial are comments that emphasize that you company is reputable and honest. And use testimonials as often as possible. Sell yourself professionally even when you are not there.

Prepare to have employees

When starting a business, I notice hiring workers may be something you do not think about. But it's amazing how quickly your business can grow and in a short while you are stalk with getting the right persons for the right job. You may decide to use contractors or employ the workforce.

Book keeping system

You will need to get your business records straight from the start. Keep clear records on what you buy and what you make. Create a budget you can work with. If you keep good records from the first moment you are starting a business, things such as accounting and paying taxes become so much easier.

Don't depend on money that is not there. Only work with what you have.

If you keep good records, accounting becomes easy. Financial records are very important to any serious-minded event planner. Invest in a quality book keeper for your business. You will save yourself time and trouble by letting someone qualified handle your finances.

Book keeping is a record of your expenses and income. When you are too busy and don't have time to do your own book keeping, consider hiring a part-time book keeper on a contract basis to do your book keeping for you. All event task has their respective cost. Some are succeeding in event planning because of high quality offering while others success can be attributed to the fact that their competitors offer poor service.

Regardless of what your plan for an event, getting a wide variety of people involve in the planning, staying organized, and keeping an open mind will bring about success. It doesn't take a hundred or a thousand people to have a grand event. It's up to you to execute exquisite and impactful event. You are not a success, without faithfully serving first your clients and secondly your community.

We should know that event service provided is more customer – driven and in most cases aim at providing convenience to the user of your service. Various choices are available to clients which should make for gingering your improvement on service quality from time to time. Financial management is short circuited without been accountable.

Accountability is often used with concepts such as answerability, responsibility, blameworthiness and liability. It is been able to make and keep agreement. It gives direction to breaking the law of extra-mile; this is delivering more than you promise to clients and guests alike.

To succeed as an event planner, you must of necessity be flexible, trustworthy and generous. This connotes doing your service to mankind as unto your creator. Your money and education are a tool to change the society not for accumulation, in which case its benefit can only accrue to you when properly managed. Always remember that you are a salesperson in this business and you serve as a company link to your clients. One means to be accountable and credible is outsourcing service. Even if you outsource you are still ultimately accountable for ensuring that the clients' needs are met. Outsourcing brings out the best in your organizing and coordinating abilities.

Consider your actions wisely before engaging money into any service supply. Be financially prudent, disciplined and fair to clients.

Financial management will help you to plan and meet clients' financial expectations through realistic projections, continuous monitoring and strict adherence to budget parameters. High customer satisfying event planners are those who provide high levels of customer service and accountability.

Policy formulation

Policies are plan of actions chosen by a business. It defines how your company will deal with employees, clients, suppliers and other important groups connected to your business.

Policies help ensure that event planners and their team act according to a legal, ethical and organizationally preferred manner of doing business.

Policies reflect on rights and responsibilities, confidentiality checks, record keeping, dress codes, evaluation, corrective actions etc.

There are policies that must of a necessity be implemented. This covers rating, charges and pricing etc.

In event planning, there are policies you can formulate which will make you outstanding as the business grows. Examples of such are:

Late request

Reservations for space should be placed at least three months in advance of any event for best results this also goes for chairs, tents etc. For any large event, I recommend more lead time. There are occasions when service cannot be provided because of several other bookings. Other times a client might be charged for overtime for service including labour and equipment. In such cases always notify your client, beforehand of the consequences of late bookings.

Cancellations

Last minute job cancellations can be costly. This is because the event planner needs to hire equipment or call professionals for an event early enough. When such late cancellation happens planners may not be able to secure another job for that weekend in question. In this situation you can charge certain percentages for jobs cancelled within twenty-four hours of the time they are scheduled to occur.

Cancellation policy is an effective way to be efficient.

Lost equipment

In event planning business lost equipment or otherwise unavailable where it is scheduled to be picked up due to breakages or losses is subject to a replacement charge equal to the full value of the equipment. To be able to buy back the lost or damaged equipment, you must incorporate this otherwise you may end up one day losing all your equipment.

Event costs

Managing the fundamentals includes earning today the cost of staying in business tomorrow. A business that does not earn these costs is bound to fade and to disappear. They are "accrued" or "deferred" costs and these are true costs that must be shown in the current accounts of a business. A business that does not earn the accrued costs of staying in business impoverishes the economy and is untrue to its first social responsibility: to maintain wealth-producing and employment producing capacities of the resources entrusted to the enterprise and its management

Event planning is an extremely difficult industry to break. It is incredibly competitive and the margins can be extremely low but that is not to say it is not a great industry to work in.

Many small businesses are successful because their overhead and income expectations are considerably lower than the competitions (overhead is the expense of a business not directly assigned to goods or services provided (monetary, time, effort or otherwise). Income is the money one earns by working or capitalizing off other people's work. Your overheads, if you are working on your own could be little. Marketing and promotions are considerations too. The biggest costs in big companies are in staff and you shouldn't have to worry too much about that during the early days.

Special event planner will establish special prices in certain seasons to draw in more customers. Just how low you can swing your rentals and printing costs will depend on your contacts.

Often there's adjustment in the basic price to accommodate differences in customers, products, locations and so on. Event planners often engage in two-part pricing consisting of a fixed fee plus a variable usage fee. They then face a problem of how much to charge for the basic service and how much for the variable usage. The fixed fee should be low enough to induce purchase of the service; the profit can then be made on the usage fees.

Throughout most of history, prices were set by negotiation between buyers and sellers. Price is the marketing-mix elements that produce revenue, the others produce cost. Price is one of the most flexible elements; it can be changed quickly.

Many small businesses are successful because their overhead and income expectations are considerably lower than the competitions. Overhead is the expense of a business not directly assigned to goods or services provided (monetary, time, effort or otherwise). Income is money one earns by working or capitalizing off other people's work.

Still others are succeeding because the competition offers poor service. It is important to ask anyone in the organization-first yourself "what do we do in this organization? And what do I do that helps you in your work"?

Many others are successful because they are first in their position with the most. The person whose business is first with the best is in an enviable position for sure.

Your supplier costs will dictate your pricings for the most part.

Price competition is the number one problem facing event planners. The clearer a firm's objectives, the easier it is to set price. Any pricing method that ignores current demand, perceived value, and competition is not likely to lead to the optimal price.

The productivity of people requires, continuous learning as the Japanese taught us. It requires that people are constantly challenged to think through what they can do to improve what they are already doing. It requires commitment on the part of the employers to anticipate redundancies and to train and place people. But above all it requires willingness to ask employees systematically and to listen to their answers. It requires acceptance of the fact that the person who does the job is likely to know more about it than the person who supervises- or at least to know different things about it.

All institutions are alike in respect to three of the four key resources- capital, time, and knowledge. These three are universal for all businesses. Event planning companies must of necessity know what the key physical resource of their businesses is. You must know approximately how many times a year your company turns over the money invested in it.

In turbulent business times, the balance sheet becomes more important than the profit and loss statement. In turbulent times it is required to know the minimum liquidity needed to stay in business. Liquidity by itself is not an objective. But in turbulent times it becomes a restraint. It becomes a survival need.

What working capital does your business need to survive a ninety –day or hundred- and twenty-day panic?

Event planners must prepare for sales and profit. In the case of non-profit organizations, it is sourcing and attracting enough funds to perform useful works; in the case of other events, the major objective is profit. There is no need to aim for profits as such but to achieve profits as a consequence of creating superior customer value.

Special event planners will offer special prices in certain seasons to draw in more customers. Often, there's adjustment in the basic price to accommodate differences in customers, products, locations and so on.

Price discrimination is legal if the planner can prove that their costs are different when selling different qualities of the same event to different buyers. Event planners often engage in two-part pricing, consisting of a fixed fee plus a variable usage fee. They then face a problem of how much to charge for basic service and how much for the variable usage. The fixed fee should be low enough to induce purchase of the service; the profit can then be made on the usage fees.

There is obvious need to get the dynamics of pricing strategy right before meeting with your client. You will have to decide how much you are going to charge for service{s} rendered, taking your competitors into consideration. Most rates are negotiable, one event planner may charge higher than the other. For example, you may need to consider the type of event, the client and how the client uses your services and the relevant accessories to be used. It is advisable to price higher when attributes such as exclusive image, standardized service or convenient location is in place. One firm visibly located can charge a slightly higher price than out - of town office.

When clients stay with your company for a number of years, prices have to be reviewed and raised for improved services that will be worth more to such customers.

Event planning is a competitive industry with high quality givers as price takers. Individual action has no effect on the market price but on your own price. Always remember that price is a means of crowd control and be moderate in your pricing.

Being able to negotiate prices for goods and services is quite essential to saving money. Saving money is the greatest value you can accord your clients. Be up-front about money.

It is imperative for you to set standards for your business and be price friendly depending on your offering, whether low quality low price, high quality low price, or high-quality high price, the choice is yours.

To some, high price equals class and uniqueness while to others low price is best sales lead. The best possible sales lead however is a satisfied client. Therefore, learn to give clients value for their money. Value, expectations and actual performance determine how satisfied your client will be. For instance, if your client places a high value on-site management and has high expectations that you will perform and you do so, you have done what is expected. You can excel with this client if you exceed the expectations, but if you do not perform, you'll have dissatisfied client.

Finding the realistic rate for a job is at times cumbersome. In some instances, while planners have to be competitive in their quotes, they also have to be constantly aware that not charging enough for services rendered will hinder their ability to hire the right people and put up as much into a client's event.

Professional business courtesy

Exercise consistent professional business courtesy to reach out to your clients/customers.

a. Give price quotes and commitments only when you know everything about the event:
b. Build lasting relationship with clients.
c. Be on time or a bit early for appointments.

Discounts

Discounts are the best instruments used to increase sales at some events. It attracts quite a number of attendees to such events examples are ticket sales for workshops, seminars, conferences, concerts and lots more. One way to stand out is to give a discount to regular customers, or perhaps a complimentary offer to first time clients. Whatever you choose to do please be consistent and make your clients want to come back to you again and again.

Competition in event planning

Competition is a fact of every business, but your ability to remember your unique assignment and work on it will make you a toast in this industry. One thing that is certain in business is that competition will continue to increase as long as we are competing for the same talent that everyone else is. There will be more people trying to render the same services as you do to the same number of people.

The wise planner will take stock of what position can be found in the marketplace by carrying out a competitor's analysis. He will need to begin by reviewing any competition. What are they doing to excel that am not doing? What is their strength, weaknesses, threat and opportunities available, then improve on them. You will need to re-examine unfulfilled human need. Is there an open niche that no one is filling? Then you find out where they are located, what they are doing per time, how many they are in your community, how many appear to be solo shops and find out what you can learn from their listings. Watch out for newspapers and relevant business publications that may feature your competitors and see what you can get to know about them. The best way to fight competition is to be sure the services you are offering match or exceed that of competitors.

This can mean the difference between a client using your services or choosing another company.

It is believed that there are two basic ways to beat competitors.

First, you must achieve superior perceived quality by developing a set of product and service standards that more closely meet customer needs than competitors. Secondly, achieve superior quality by being more effective than your competitors.

Never compromise today's trend as this can help to win great businesses. To win competition, you need to gain confidence by learning absolutely everything about the services and be willing to convince clients of the relevance of your service in solving their problems. You can outwit your competitors through adequate planning.

A business needs to be at least as efficient as its main competitors in order to be able to compete and survive in the long term.

If you are targeting corporate market, your competition will consist not only of other event planning entrepreneurs, but also of in-house protocol staff hired by corporations to oversee meetings and events. Many corporations choose to outsource event planning responsibility to keep costs low. In the social event your main competitors will be other event planning entrepreneurs as well as caterers, decorators who have taken on the responsibilities of planning events as a sideline fun.

Find out the elements which are important to customers, how well competitors perform them, and how well you are perceived to perform them. Bear in mind that customers taste is constantly changing and this brings challenges and opportunities to you and your competitors alike. To therefore increase your competitive capacity, you need a solid positioning that will differentiate you from competitors in your line of business and conceptualization. When you do this long enough and strongly too you will eventually develop to the point that customers cannot help but to look for you.

Healthy competition is very good for any business, don't be scared of a lot of competition instead look for a niche you can fill and think about what will make your event planning company stand out in the crowd.

If you strive to be the best, research your market, promote yourself, develop good business plan and you will find your spot in the market place.

Perhaps you don't dare to sell your product because you don't want to be rejected.

You may want to know the following about your competitors:

    a. Services they offer and how they are reaching their target market

    b. Do they advertise, if not you can quickly use this medium.

c.   Are they at the focal point of community issues or not.
d.   How do they promote and execute events?

Figure out a way to set yourself apart from your competitors. You may set yourself apart in marketing, networking, service offering. Be precise, pay attention to details, and be vast in learning about your competitive advantage. Competitive advantage is gained by finding an aspect of differentiation that targeted customers will perceive as superior value and that cannot be easily duplicated by competitors. A.P. Akpan in his book enumerated these examples to include:

a.   Superior image benefits
b.   Superior service benefits in all service offerings
c.   Superior customer relationships and interpersonal abilities
d.   Effective marketing advantages

What is your sustainable competitive advantage? By this I mean your ability to know your core competence as well as your unique selling proposition. Core competencies are areas of special technical and production expertise and capabilities that tend to describe excellence. Capabilities tend to describe excellence in a broader term. Your core competencies position you positively. There is need to maintain your competitive positioning through efficient service delivery because it makes you a high flyer. Be difficult for competitors to imitate.

Spend most of your time on vendor consultations, networking, bookkeeping and event design. Go to staff meetings once a week, conduct on –site supervision, consult with clients and route deliveries to event venues.

Chapter Fifteen

Attitudinal change

The impossible many times is just simply the untried. Every great idea will first seem to be impossible until you do something with it. Our comfort zones hold us back from unleashing the potentials we know we have.

Change is inevitable and it takes strong willed heart to effect a positive change. We need to leave our comfort zones and embrace a paradigm shift. Let us consider an analogy, suppose for instance you want to learn to play a musical instrument.

Your instruction might begin with several classes and reading assignments about your particular instrument and descriptions of the various parts of the instrument and their functions. Sooner or later, however, you would have actually played the instrument. Eventually you become an accomplished musician. The same is applicable here. Make the right statement with every event you help in creating. Though the fear of being different prevents most people from seeking new ways of doing things.

Right attitude is the starting point of all business and event planning is no exception. It is highly significant that the creator provided man with control over nothing except the power to shape our thoughts and the privilege of fitting the thoughts to any pattern of our choice. You must recognize your right to exist and understand the power of self – assertiveness within the boundaries of purposefulness and integrity. Be a possibility thinking expert. A possibility thinking expert is a person who when faced with a new business concept and knowing that it has never been successfully implemented is charged with excitement at what he sees as a greater opportunity to discover new solutions to old problems using knowledge of new age to make historic breakthrough. Delete the word impossible out of your vocabulary. Impossible is a roadblock to progress. Become possibility conscious and make a deliberate decision to develop a positive attitude toward opportunities and obstacles.

I am of the opinion that regardless of the dwindling market situation and the financial crisis, your attitude can give you a competitive edge. The more positive you are, the better your life will be in every area. Your speed of performance is dependent on how well you can see. I know this is why we were created with a plan to keep growing non-stop.

Keep your thoughts on your dreams, goals and aspirations as it has to do with the business. It is possible to be cheerful and put smiles on the faces of customers and those around you. This has made me realize that something on the inside is what makes life on the outside work best. The purpose of every business is to create and keep clients with uniqueness; therein making profit becomes inevitable.

As the chief executive owner of the business always see yourself as the number one salesperson of the company. Only through this process can you gain access to people and win them over. The Jews in the days of Esther faced serious challenges but a day came and they got their victory, so it is for any business. You cannot get success without exchanging words with failure. But in failure, think your way out to success. The horses and chariots on the way should not deter your commitment.

Your little beginning should not be a source of discouragement. If you do it today and it doesn't work try again and never give up. Remain useful, consistent and undeterred. In this business, getting people to entrust their budget may seem hard, but keep at it and with your persistence it will pay off. You will therefore need patience as an essential for success in event planning. Increase self-confidence and have faith in your ability to achieve greatness, bearing in mind that there is no born event planner. Self-confidence is not a byproduct of drugs and it is not enhanced by drugs. It is essentially who you are on the inside without external forces having any influence. The magic word confidence works wonder, it will roll out red carpets for you, it will connect you to some of the most beautiful and powerful people in the business world. If a positive self- image is lacking so will be the confidence that problems in business can be solved or managed creatively.

Remember you are in event business as predestined by God except you are out copying only what others are doing. It is only natural to give recognition to your source as the only true builder of your business. Become confidently aware of the positioning principle in marketing.

Our peculiar nature is not contacted by social status but rather, made available to us by divine power which means your dreams can be a reality. Never use the word impossible or assess yourself on the basis of connections or background. There are some ideas on your inside; the ability to accept them and get them refined will take you places.

Never under-estimate or over-estimate yourself, just be your unique self and see things working out as predestined.

Choose making a deliberate decision to develop the right attitude towards obstacles and opportunities. There are many giants in our world today that ought to be killed in our businesses. Negative thinking and self- pity are some of the giants which can be conquered by re-conditioning the mind. Fear not that you might fail, fear rather that you might never succeed if you never dare to try. Problems are okay! They only prove that you are living and growing and very human. Business Problems? If we hadn't chosen to go into business in the first place, we wouldn't have problems. Failures are only problems waiting to be solved. You can choose how you will react to what happens to you. The first step to survival is this: Do Nothing. When every other element to of a problem is out of your control, remember you can still manage your reaction! Positive thinkers know that though times never last but though people do.

Surround yourself with people who can help you actualize your goals. Keep company with the wise, get employees skilled in the business. No wonder our Life reference book says iron sharpens iron. See challenges and not problems. Every challenge is temporal, it will have its peak and then it's downhill all the way. Make your dream big enough for your source of existence to fit in. A big dream is one which is so large that it requires the almighty to make it come true. Success does not happen until you involve the true source of success. Determine that you are going to make your dream as an event planner happen, it may appear impossible, but move ahead and get definite about what you want.

Everyone who is doing well today was once doing poorly. You attract into your life, the people, the circumstances, the opportunities, and even the clients that are in harmony with your dominant thoughts. As you change your thinking about yourself and your possibilities, you can change your life and rule your world. Think more on being a goal getter and be more enthusiastic and excited about life.

Don't become negative when people haven't given you adequate recognition. Somehow your business will have to be successfully marketed to make sure that people who would benefit from your creativity know that your contribution is actually available to them.

The wise possibility thinker will take stock of what position can be found in the marketplace. He will begin by reviewing any competition. What are they doing to excel that am not doing? What is their strength, weakness, threats and opportunities, then find ways to improve on them. Then you will need to re-examine unfulfilled human need. Is there an open niche that no one else is filling? You will need to alter your course. Even if somebody has your position in the marketplace wrapped up, don't discard your plan of doing something differently.

The most important single quality for great success in business is the virtue of optimism. Be optimistic and have high aspirations. See yourself as capable of being the best event planner in your locality. Abraham Lincoln said it best: "whatever you are, be a good one."

Make a decision that you are going to be excellent and then take actions to learn and apply whatever knowledge and skills you need to get ahead and stay on top by putting one foot ahead in front of the other foot. The turning point in your life is to make a decision, clear, unequivocal decision that you are going to be the best and then follow your decision with precision and determination until you reach your goal.

The potential customer may not like your policies, or how you go about your business but when you put confidence in place, you will know and understand better that negative attitude is counterproductive.

Once a customer views you as a professional and a friend, you will be the only one they go to. See yourself more as the event planner, walk, talk, and behave like a problem solver.

It is very important to note that whatever you think of yourself counts much more than what you believe others think of you.

It is more advantageous to think, act and build your business on the premix of uniqueness. If you can change your way of thinking then you can change your business.

Discipline is key to success. Discipline your thought and your action. There is an old saying that "a thousand wishes won't fill a basket with fishes."

Glossary

ATTITUDE: A state of mind or feeling of an individual, group or society regarding issues such as material gain, hard-work, saving for the future, sharing wealth etc.

COMPARATIVE ADVANTAGE: A business has a comparative advantage over another if in producing its services it can do so at a relatively lower opportunity cost in terms of the forgone alternative commodities that could be produced.

COORDINATION FAILURE: A state of affairs in which the planners' inability to coordinate their choices leads to an outcome (equilibrium) that leaves all guests worse off than in an alternative that is also an equilibrium.

DEADLINE: the point in time at which something must be completed

EQUILIBRIUM PRICE: The price at which the quantity demanded of a good is exactly equal to the quantity supplied.

HUMAN RESOURCE: The quality and quantity of labour force in a nation or an organization.

IMPERFECT COMPETITION: A market situation or structure in which producers have some degree of control over the price of their product.

IMPERFECT MARKET: A market where theoretical assumptions of perfect competition are violated by the existence of, for example, a small number of buyers and sellers, barriers to entry and incomplete information.

INCOME GAP: The gap between the incomes accruing to the bottom (poor) and the top (rich) sectors of a population. When we have a wider gap, the inequality in the income distribution becomes greater.

MODEL: An analytical framework used to portray functional relationships among economic factors.

PARADIGM: Implicit assumptions from which theories evolve; a model or framework of analysis.

PRICE: The monetary or real value of a resource, commodity or service. It is the role of prices in a market economy to ration or allocate resources in accordance with supply and demands.

PROFIT: The difference between the market value of output and the market value of inputs employed to produce the output. It is also the difference between total revenue and total cost.

RISK: A situation in which the probability of obtaining some outcome of an event is not precisely known.

SELF RELIANCE: Reliance on one's own capabilities, judgment, resources and skills in a bid to enhance political, economic, social, cultural, attitudinal and moral independence.

SERVICE: Economic activities other than industry and primary goods production.

SHADOW PRICE: This is a price that reflects the true opportunity cost of a resource.

TASK: This is a piece of work done as part of one's duties.

UNCERTAINTY: A situation in which the probability of obtaining a given outcome of an event is not known.

VALUES: Principles, standards or qualities considered worthwhile or desirable.

VALUE ADDED: Amount of product or services final value added at each stage of production.

VICIOUS CYCLE: A self – reinforcing situation in which factors tend to perpetuate a certain undesirable phenomenon.

Reference

ASTA BELOVIENE ET AL.

Event Management Handbook

A.B. AKPAN (PHD).

Industrial Marketing Management Buyers and Sellers, 2002

BILL NEWMAN.

10 Laws of leadership,1997

DALE CARNEGIE.

How to Win Friends and Influence People: Copyright, 1936.

FABJOB.COM.

Become an event planner. Copyright 2002

GARY, FELLERS.

How to be a Creative Thinker: Pelican Publishing, 1996

GLEEN BOWDIN et al.

Event Management. 2nd Edition, Page 294-317

JOHN W. STANKO.

Strictly Business: 2002

JOE LOCICERO

Meeting and Event Planning (2007)

MICHEAL P. TODARO & STEPHEN C. SMITH

Economic Development (2006; pages: 13-33)

MYLES MUNROE.

The burden of freedom (2006)

PETER F. DRUCKER

Managing in turbulent times (1980)

PHILIP KOTLER.

Marketing management (2001)

RICH G. LIPSEY.

An introduction to Positive Economics

ROBERT KREITNER

Management sixth edition (1995; pages: 410-411)

Discover this book

Events are a constant in our lives, yet only a few planners consistently achieve success. What sets them apart? The right knowledge, mentorship, and strategies. If you're serious about building a profitable event planning business, you need a clear roadmap to guide you.

In Professional Event Planning: A Complete Skill-Building Guide, Dr. Mandy Adebayo, a seasoned event consultant with decades of experience, shares her proven methods for success. With an impressive portfolio of corporate and social events, Dr. Mandy breaks down the essentials needed to thrive, even in challenging markets.

This handbook provides step-by-step guidance, transforming you into a sought-after event planner. You'll learn how to:

- Build and grow your event planning business.
- Develop a personalized planning model.
- Seamlessly organize and execute successful events.
- Implement effective strategies for maximum results.

Each chapter tackles crucial areas like business strategy, marketing, risk management, and event evaluation. Whether you're new to event planning or aiming to refine your skills, this book delivers the tools you need to succeed.

Professional Event Planning is an indispensable guide for event planners, managers, and entrepreneurs looking to elevate their careers. With Dr. Mandy's insights, you'll gain the knowledge and confidence to turn your event planning business into a profitable venture.

Ready to take your career to the next level? This book will equip you with everything you need to succeed.